THE STANDARD

ANTIQUE DOLL

IDENTIFICATION & VALUE GUIDE
1700 - 1935

COVER DOLL
KAMMER & REINHARDT POUTY

Copyright: Bill Schroeder, 1976
ISBN: 0-89145-014-9

COLLECTOR BOOKS
P. O. Box 3009
Paducah, Kentucky 42001

DEDICATION

The editors to the Schroeder Publishing Company dedicate this volume to all collectors and dealers who not only want to know WHAT the doll is but also want to know it's VALUE.

ACKNOWLEDGEMENTS

The editors wish to thank the following for the use of their doll's pictures: Jane Alton, Helen Draves, Maxine Heitt, Thelma Flack, Kimport Dolls, Jay Minter, Grace Orschner, Mary Partridge and R. H. Stevens.

PRICING

The prices in this book are meant to be a GUIDE, not absolute prices as, on pricing dolls, much depends on the CONDITION as well as what a collector is willing to pay.

If your doll is <u>less</u> than PERFECT, deduct amount from these prices accordingly. A PERFECT doll is one that is clean and all there, with <u>no</u> cracks, nicks, chips, breaks, fingers or toes gone or bad scuffs. BUT ESPECIALLY NO hairline cracks, breaks, chips from the heads.

CONTENTS

4

Bru: 1885. Bisque swivel head. Closed mouth. Cork pate. White bisque. Kid body. Gusseted. MARKS: Bebe BRU/SGDG. 16" $2,600.00

Bru: 1881. Bisque swivel head. Open mouth. Knob on back of head. MARKS: Bebe Gourmand. 20" $2,350.00

Bru: 1891. Bisque swivel head. Open closed mouth. Inset eyes. Compo. body. Walks and talks. MARKS: Bebe Petit Pas. 23" $2,150.00

Bru: 1879. Bisque swivel head. Open mouth. Inset eyes. Pierced ears. Mache body. Nursing Bru. MARKS: Bebe Teteur. 20" $2,650.00

Bru: Bisque swivel. Open closed mouth. Inset eyes. Kid body. Gusseted bisque forearms. MARKS: BRU Jne/O. 14" $2,600.00

Bru: Bisque shoulder head. Closed mouth. Kid body. Bisque forearms. MARKS: BRU Jne. 16" $2,850.00

Bru: 3 faces (smile, tears, sleep) changed by head knob. Cloth body. Compo hands and feet. MARKS: BRU Jne CB. $1,800.00

Bru: Bisque swivel head. Open mouth. Inset eyes. Pierced ears. Compo body. Strings for doll to raise hand and throw Kiss. Baby. MARKS: BRU Jne. 20" $1,950.00

Bru: Bisque swivel head. Open mouth. Inset eyes. Kid body. Kid over wood upper arms. Bisque forearms. Wooden fore-legs. MARKS: Bru Jne/8. 20" $3,900.00

Bru: Bisque swivel head. Open closed mouth. Inset eyes. Pierced ears. Kid body. Kid covered wood joints. MARKS: BRU Jne/6/circle dot. 18" $3,800.00

Bru: Bisque swivel. Open closed mouth. Goat skin hair. Compo body. MARKS: BRU Jne/2. 16" $2,000.00

Bru: Bisque swivel head. Open mouth. Inset eyes. Pierced ears. Compo body. MARKS: BRU Jne/3. 18" $1,600.00

Bru: Bisque swivel head. Open closed mouth. Inset eyes. Pierced ears. Wooden body. Joints have wood pegs. MARKS: BRU Jne/5. 20" $3,800.00

Bru: Bisque swivel head. Open mouth. Mohair. Pierced ears. Kid body. Molded bosom. Bisque forearms. MARKS: BRU Jne/6t. 23" $2,900.00

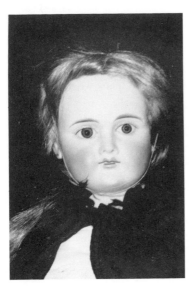

BELTON

20" Socket head on fully jointed composition/wood body. Closed mouth. Set blue eyes. Pierced ears. Flat top with 3 holes. $695.00

BELTON

14" Socket head with composition and wood body. Full joints except wrists. Pierced ears. Closed mouth. Flat top with 2 holes. $650.00

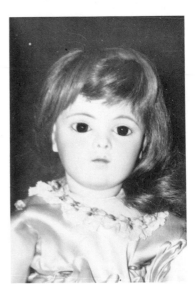

BRU

14" Swivel neck shoulder plate. Pierced ears. Closed mouth. Kid over wood body, upper arms & legs. Wood lower legs. Bisque lower arms. MARKS: BRU JNE 4. $3,500.00

BRU

17" Swivel neck shoulder plate. Kid over wood body and limbs with bisque lower arms. Pierced ears & closed mouth. MARKS: BRU JNE/5. $3,695.00

6

Fleischmann & Bloedel: 1890. Bisque swivel head. Closed mouth. Inset eyes. Wig. Kid body. Bisque hands. MARKS: Eden. Bebe/Paris. 21" $1,050.00

Fleischmann & Bloedel: Bisque swivel head. Closed mouth. Inset eyes. Pierced ears. Compo body. MARKS: Eden Bebe PARIS L. 30" $1,300.00

Fleischmann & Bloedel: Bisque swivel head. Open mouth. Inset eyes. Pierced ears. Compo body. MARKS: Eden Bebe PARIS M. 21" $600.00

F. Gaultier.   Bisque shoulder head. Closed mouth. Inset eyes. Pierced ears. Gesland body of stockinet. Bisque hands. MARKS: F. G. 29" $1,450.00

Gaultier, F.:   Fashion. Bisque swivel head. Closed mouth. Inset eyes. Pierced ears. Kid body. Gussetted. Wooden hands. MARKS: F.G/4. 13" $550.00

Gaultier, F.:   Bisque swivel head. Closed mouth. Inset eyes. Rose tint eye shadow. Gesland stamped body of stockinet. MARKS: F. 10 G. 16" $1,100.00

Jullien, Jr.:   Bisque head. Closed mouth. Inset eyes. Compo body. MARKS: Jullien JJ 2278. 20" $1,200.00

Jumeau: Bisque swivel head. Closed mouth. Inset eyes. Long curls. Pierced ears. Compo body. MARKS: Depose/Tete Jumeau/Bte SGDG /2. 18" $995.00

Jumeau: Bisque swivel head. Closed mouth. Inset eyes. Kid body marked "Jumeau, Medaille d'Or, Paris". Gussetted. MARKS: E 3 J. 20" $1,300.00

Jumeau: Bisque swivel head. Closed mouth. Inset eyes. Kid body. MARKS: E 6 J/Jumeau. 16" $1,050.00

Jumeau: Bisque swivel head. Closed mouth. Inset eyes. Pierced ears. Compo body. MARKS: Depose/Tete Jumeau/Bte SGDG/8. 28" $1,300.00

Jumeau: Bisque swivel head. Closed mouth. Inset eyes. Compo body. "mama" and "Papa" strings. MARKS: Jumeau/10/Brevete SGDG. 16" $995.00

Jumeau: Bisque swivel head. Open mouth. Compo body. MARKS: Jumeau 301 11. 21" $500.00

Jumeau: Bisque swivel head. Open mouth. Inset eyes. Pierced ears. Compo body. Called "The Screamer". MARKS: 211/Jumeau/check mark. 17" $2,500.00

E. DENAMUR

32" Socket head with fully jointed composition & Wood body. Pierced ears. Closed mouth. Large blue set eyes. MARKS: E 14 D/DEPOSE. 32" $1,400.00

FLEISCHMANN & BLODEL

23" Socket head on fully jointed composition/wood body. Open mouth, pierced ears. MARKS: EDEN BEBE/PARIS/10/DEPOSE. $600.00

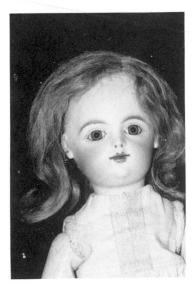

GAULTIER, F.

13" Socket head on composition & wood body. Pierced ears. Blue paperweight eyes. Closed mouth. MARKS: F.G., in scroll. $995.00

GAULTIER, F.

15" Fashion. Kid body. Shoulder plate. Swivel neck bisque head. Glass blue eyes. Closed mouth. Ears are pierced. MARKS: F.G. $595.00

Jumeau: Bisque swivel head. Open mouth. Sleep eyes. Pierced ears. Compo body. MARKS: Jumeau 1907. 18" $400.00

Jumeau: Bisque swivel head. Open mouth. Inset eyes. Pierced ears. Compo body. MARK: Jumeau 1909. 21" $495.00

Lanternier, A. and Co.:   Bisque swivel head. Closed mouth. Inset eyes. Cloth body. Voice box. Weighted metal feet. MARKS: A. Lanternier & Co/Limoges. 16" $300.00

Lanternier A. & Co.:   Bisque shoulder head. Open closed mouth. Sleep eyes. Compo body. MARKS: J. E. Maston SC/Lorraine N AL/Co/Limoges. 23" $400.00

Lanternier, A. & Co.:   Bisque shoulder head. Open mouth. Sleep eyes. MARKS: J. E. Maston SC/Lorraine No AL&Co/Limoges. 16" $375.00

SFBJ: Bisque swivel head. Closed mouth. Inset eyes. Pierced ears. Compo body. MARKS: Tete Depose/Paris Bebe/SFBJ 11. 16" $595.00

SFBJ: Bisque swivel head. Open mouth. Inset eyes. Mache body. MARKS: Celestine/SFBJ. 18" $400.00

SFBJ: Bisque socket head. Open mouth. Inset eyes. Compo body. MARKS: 25/FRANCE/SFBJ/301/PARIS. 16" $250.00

SFBJ: 1900. Bisque head. Open closed mouth. Laughing. Inset eyes. Wig. Compo body. MARKS: 21/SFBJ/60/PARIS 8. 20" $695.00

SFBJ: Bisque swivel head. Closed mouth. Smile Inset eyes. Compo body. MARKS: SFBJ/203/PARIS. $1,050.00

SFBJ: Bisque swivel head. Closed mouth. Inset eyes. Side glance. Compo body. MARKS: SFBJ/215/PARIS. $1,050.00

SFBJ: Bisque head. Closed dome. Molded hair. Open closed mouth. Smile. Inset eyes. Character face. Compo body. Wooden joints. MARKS: SFBJ/226/PARIS. 20" $950.00

SFBJ: Bisque head. Closed dome. Open mouth. Inset eyes. Painted hair. Smile. Compo body. MARKS: SFBJ/227/PARIS. $950.00

SFBJ: Brown bisque swivel head. Closed dome. Animal skin wig. Open mouth. Inset eyes. Compo body. MARKS: SFBJ/227/PARIS. $1,250.00

9

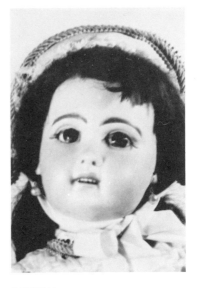

GAULTIER, F.

15" Socket head. Composition & wood body. Set blue eyes. Closed mouth. MARKS: F. G. $975.00

JUMEAU

23" Composition & wood body. Bisque head with large brown eyes. Open mouth. MARKS: 1907. 23" $495.00

JUMEAU

18" Composition & wood body. Bisque head with set eyes, pierced ears and open mouth. MARKS: 1907. $400.00

JUMEAU

17" Socket head. Large set eyes. Pierced ears. Closed mouth. Completely original. MARKS: TETE JUMEAU, on head. JUMEAU/ MEDAL D'or/PARIS, in body. $950.00

SFBJ: Bisque head. Closed mouth. Inset eyes. Smile. Mache body. Toddler/MARKS: SFBJ/228/PARIS. 16" $995.00

SFBJ.   Bisque swivel head. Closed mouth. Inset eyes. Smile. Wooden body. Walks. MARKS: SFBJ/229/PARIS 8. 18" $1,050.00

SFBJ: Bisque swivel head. Open closed mouth. Inset eyes. Compo body. Non-walker. MARKS: SFBJ/229/PARIS. 18" $1,050.00

SFBJ: Bisque head. Open mouth. Inset eyes. Pierced ears. Compo body. Walks. MARKS: Tete Jumeau/SFBJ 230/PARIS. 16" $695.00

SFBJ: Bisque head. Closed dome. Open mouth. Inset eyes. 8 teeth. Molded hair. MARKS: SFBJ/233/PARIS. 17" $1,800.00

SFBJ: Bisque head. Closed dome. Molded hair. Open closed mouth. Sleep eyes. Laughing. Compo body. MARKS: SFBJ/235/PARIS. 18" $950.00

SFBJ: Called "Laughing Jumeau". Bisque swivel head. Open mouth. Sleep eyes. Tongue. Double chin. Compo body. MARKS: SFBJ/236 /PARIS. 18" $950.00

SFBJ: Bisque swivel head. Closed dome. Molded hair. Closed mouth. Inset eyes. Mache body. MARKS: SFBJ 237 PARIS/Poulbot. 16" $2,200.00

SFBJ: Bisque swivel head. Open mouth. Inset eyes. Compo body. MARKS: SFBJ/238/PARIS 6. 21" $995.00

SFBJ: Mache head. Closed mouth. Inset eyes. Googlie looking up. Mache body. MARKS: SFBJ 245/28/0/PARIS. 12" $750.00

SFBJ: Bisque swivel head. Closed mouth. Inset eyes. Pouty. Character face. Mache body. MARKS: SFBJ/252/PARIS. 22" $2,500.00

SFBJ: Bisque swivel head. Open closed mouth. Inset eyes. Compo body. MARKS: SFBJ/247/PARIS. 24" $1,800.00

SFBJ: 1900. Bisque swivel head. Open closed mouth. Sleep eyes. Tongue. Hair lashes. Dimples. Character baby. Compo body. MARKS: SFBJ/251/PARIS. 16" $800.00

SFBJ: 1900. Bisque head. Open closed mouth. Inset eyes. Toddler. Compo body. MARKS: SFBJ/257/PARIS. 16" $1,050.00

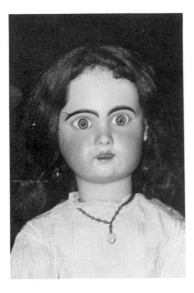

JUMEAU

33″ Socket head on composition & wood body. Applied ears. Open mouth. 19½″ head circumference. MARKS: 15, incised on head. 33″ $750.00

JUMEAU

32″ Socket head on composition & wood body. Open mouth. Applied ears. MARKS: 1907. Has an 18″ head circumference. 32″ $750.00

JUMEAU

20″ Mache & composition body. Bisque head has paperweight eyes, pierced ears & closed mouth. MARKS: E.J./DEPOSE. Body: JUMEAU/MEDAL D'or/PARIS. 20″ $1,300.00

JUMEAU

13″ Shoulder head on kid body with bisque forearms. Bald head with set eyes and closed mouth. MARKS: 639 No.6. Made for Jumeau by Kestner. 13″ $325.00

12

Steiner: Bisque swivel head. Open mouth. Wire works sleep eyes. Compo body. MARKS: STE C-1/(head stamp) Steiner Bte SGDG/ Bourgoin PARIS. 18" $1,300.00

Steiner: Bisque swivel head. Closed mouth. Eyes wired for sleep. Pierced ears. Compo body. Voice by pull string. MARKS: Steiner Bte SGDG/Bourgoin STE C-5. 25" $1,500.00

Steiner: Bisque swivel head. Closed mouth. Eyes. Wired for sleep. Compo body. MARKS: STE SGDG SIE/A 5 Bourgoin SR. 23" $1,400.00

Steiner: Bisque swivel head. Closed mouth. Inset eyes. Pierced ears. Compo body. MARKS: Steiner PARIS/Bte SGDG/F AE A 9. 17" $1,295.00

Steiner: Bisque swivel head. Closed mouth. Inset eyes. Compo body. MARKS: Steriner PARIS/Bte A10. 19" $1,395.00

Steiner: Bisque swivel head. Closed mouth. Inset eyes. Pierced ears. Compo body. Baby. MARKS: Steiner PARIS/F A 12. 20" $1,400.00

Steiner: Bisque swivel head. Open mouth. Inset eyes. Compo body. String for "Mama". MARKS: Steiner PARIS/A 119. 18" $1,395.00

Steiner: Bisque swivel head. Closed mouth. Inset eyes. Compo body. MARKS: Steiner PARIS/Bte SGDG/F 1 AE A 18. 26" $1,500.00

Steiner: Bisque swivel head. Closed mouth. Inset eyes. Pierced ears. Mache body. MARKS: J. Steiner PARIS/Bte SGDG/A 5. 16" $1,295.00

Steiner: Bisque swivel head. Closed mouth. Inset eyes. Pierced ears. Compo body. MARKS: J. Steiner PARIS/LE PARISIEN/F 1 AE A 11. 19" $1,395.00

Steiner: Brown bisque head. Closed mouth. Inset eyes. Compo body. MARKS: J. Steiner/PARIS A 7. 16" Colored $1,800.00

Steiner: White bisque head. Open closed mouth. Inset eyes. Compo body. Wooden limbs. MARKS: J. Steiner PARIS/Bte SGDG/F 1 AE A 19. 28" $1,500.00

Steiner: Bisque swivel head. Closed mouth. Inset eyes. Pierced ears. Compo body. MARKS: J. Steiner PARIS/LE PARISIEN/F 1 AE A 11. 19" $1,395.00

Steiner: Bisque head. Closed mouth. Inset eyes. Compo body. MARKS: J. Steiner PARIS/Bte SGDG/F 1 AE A 13. 21" $1,400.00

LANTERNIER

13" Socket head with composition full jointed body. Bisque head with open mouth/molded teeth. Sleep eyes/lashes. MARKS: FABRICATION FRANCOISE/LIMOGES/FRANCE/T.B./4. $195.00

PARIS BEBE

17" Socket head on fully jointed composition & wood body. Closed mouth. Set eyes. MARKS: PARIS BEBE/TETE DEPOSEE/7. Eiffel Tower stamp on body. $1,195.00

STEINER, JULES NICKOLS

10" Bisque head with closed mouth. Mache "stick" type body. MARKS: STEINER/PARIS/Fr A-3. $595.00

STEINER, JULES NICKOLS

25" Composition & wood body. Bisque head with closed mouth. Set paperweight eyes. Pierced ears. MARKS: A17/PARIS(incised)/LePARISIEN/ SGDG stamped in red. $1,500.00

Thuillier, A.:   Bisque swivel head. Open mouth. Clockwork in head moves eyes. Mache body. MARKS: A T. 20" $5,000.00

Thuillier, A.:   Bisque swivel head. Closed mouth. Pierced ears. White bisque. Kid body. MARKS: A 5 T. 16" $4,700.00

Thuillier, A.:   Bisque swivel head. Open mouth. Compo body. MARKS: A 8 T. 19" $5,000.00

Thuillier, A.:   Bisque swivel head. Closed mouth. Inset eyes. Pierced ears. Wooden body. MARKS: A T No. 8. 20" $5,200.00

Thuillier, A.:   White bisque swivel head. Closed mouth. Inset eyes. Pierced ears. Mache body. Adult body. MARKS: A 12 T. 24" $7,000.00

Schmitt&fils: 1879. Bisque swivel head. Closed mouth. Inset eyes. Pierced ears. Cork Pate. Compo body. Marked "Bebe Schmitt". MARKS: Bte (SCH & crossed hammers in shield) SGDG/0. 16" $1,500.00

Schmitt&fils: 1879. Bisque swivel head. Closed mouth. Inset eyes. Compo body. Body stamped "Bebe Schmitt". MARKS: Bte (SCH & crossed hammers in shield) SGDG. 18" $1,700.00

Schmitt&fils: Bisque swivel head. Closed mouth. Inset eyes. Mache body stamped "Bebe Schmitt". MARKS: Bte (SCH & crossed hammers in shield) SGDG. 20" $1,900.00

Simonne, F.:   White bisque swivel head. Closed mouth. Inset eyes. Kid body. Bisque forearms. MARKS: Passage Delorme/No. 1 a 13/ Rue DeRivoli 188. (in oval). 12" $675.00

Simonne, F.:   Bisque swivel head. Closed mouth. Inset eyes. Gray. Kid body. Bisque forearms. MARKS: Passage Delorme/SIMONNE/ Rue DeRivoli 188. (in oval). 18" $950.00

Mme. Rohmer: Bisque swivel head. Closed mouth. Painted eyes. Kid body. Kid covers wood. Bisque forearms. MARKS: Mme. Rohmer/ Brevete SGDG A Paris (in oval). 14" $3,000.00

UNIS: Bisque swivel head. Open mouth. Sleep eyes. Tongue. Compo body. MARKS: UNIS France 251. 18" $350.00

UNIS: Mache shoulder head. Mohair. Mache body. MARKS: UNIS France 251. 18" $150.00

UNIS: Bisque swivel head. Open closed mouth. Inset eyes. Mache body. Metal arms and hands paper wrapped. Rocks a baby and kissed it. MARKS: 71 UNIS FRANCE/301. 149/2. 14" $500.00

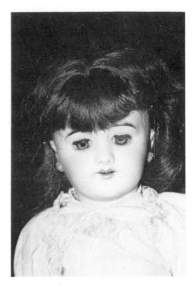

STEINER, JULES
20" Bisque head. Open mouth/2
rows teeth. Kid, composition &
cartouche body. Keywind, doll
moves arms, kicks feet and head
turns & she cries. Lambs wool
wig. $1,295.00

S. F. B. J.
18" Composition body. Bisque
head with pierced ears, sleep eyes
/lashes and an open mouth. MA-
RKS: DEPOSEE/S.F.B.J./TETE
JUMEAU. $575.00

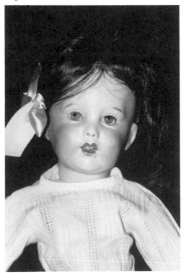

S. F. B. J.

13" Socket head with composition
full jointed body. Sleep blue eyes.
Open mouth/tongue. MARKS: S.F.
B.J. 251/PARIS/4. $650.00

S. F. B. J.

15" Socket head with composition body with straight legs. Straight
arms molded in a curve. Open
mouth. MARKS: S.F.B.J./60/PAR-
IS. $175.00

Lefebvre, Alexandre: Mache head. Mache body. Joints permit sitting and kneeling. MARKS: Bebe A.L. 18'' $850.00

Rabery & Delphieu: 1898. Bisque swivel head. Closed mouth. Inset eyes. Compo body. Walks & talks. MARKS: Bebe de Paris/R.D./3. 18'' $900.00

Jumeau, E.:   1896. Bisque swivel head. Closed mouth. Inset eyes. Compo body. MARKS: Bebe Francois. 18'' $995.00

Jumeau, E.:   Bisque swivel head. Closed mouth. Inset eyes. Smile. Dimples. Pierced ears. Compo body with mark "Diploma d'Honneur". MARKS: Bebe Jumeau 224. 18'' $1,050.00

May Freres: 1890. Bisque swivel head. Closed mouth. Inset eyes. Compo body. MARKS: M7 (head)/Mascotte. Bebe Mascotte/Paris. (body). 20'' $995.00

Steiner: 1899. Bisque head. Closed mouth. Inset eyes. Compo body. MARKS: Bebe Liege. 18'' $1,350.00

Steiner: 1901. Bisque head. Closed mouth. Inset eyes. Compo body. MARKS: Bebe Modele. 18'' $1,350.00

Schnitz, P.H.:   Bisque head. Closed mouth. Inset eyes. Compo body. MARKS: Bebe Moderne. 18'' $950.00

SFBJ: 1902. Bisque head. Closed mouth. Inset eyes. Compo body. MARKS: Bebe Parisiana. 18'' $650.00

Alexandre, Henri: 1890. Bisque swivel head. Closed mouth. Inset eyes. Pierced ears. Compo body. MARKS: Bebe Phenix/Articule Brevette/SGDG No. 13. 23'' $1,250.00

Jumeau, E.:   1893. Bisque head. Open mouth. Compo body. Body mechanism permitted changing music cylinders through French, English, & Spanish. MARKS: Bebe Phonographe. 18'' $700.00

Rabery & Delphieu: Bisque swivel head. Closed mouth. Inset eyes. Compo body. MARKS: Bebe Rabery (body stamp) (head) R.D. 18'' $950.00

Fleischmann & Blodel: 1898. They were German and had factories in Germany and France. Bisque heads. MARKS: Bebe Triomphe. Closed mouth. 18'' $900.00

S. F. B. J.

11" Socket head with mache/compo. body. One piece body and legs. Plunger type cryer. Open mouth. MARKS: SFBJ/60/PARIS. $200.00

S. F. B. J.

12" Socket head with mache & wood body. Sleep pale blue eyes. Open mouth. Original clothes. MARKS: SFBJ/60. $185.00

UNIS

14½" Brown bisque socket head on brown full jointed compo. body. Set eyes and open mouth. Ears unpierced. Large earrings sewn to hair. Original. MARKS: UNIS FRANCE/60. $395.00

UNIS

12" Five piece composition body. Bisque head with open mouth/4 teeth. Set blue eyes. Blonde mohair. Original clothes. MARKS: 71 UNIS/FRANCE, in oval /149 /60. $350.00

Alt. Beck & Gottschalk: Bisque socket head. Open mouth/teeth. Sleep eyes. Compo. body. Voice box. Baby. MARKS: ABG (in scroll)/1352 /B2 GERMANY 16" $165.00

Alt. Beck & Gottschalk: Bisque socket head. Open mouth. Sleep eyes. Spring strung wooden body. MARKS: ABG(in scroll)/1361/GER-MANY 13" $150.00

Alt. Beck & Gottschalk: Bisque head baby. Open mouth. Sleep eyes. Pierced nostrils. Compo. body. MARKS: ABG (in scroll)/1361/GER-MANY 18" $185.00

Alt. Beck & Gottschalk: Bisque socket head. Open mouth. Sleep eyes. Lashes. 2 holes in back of head. Pierced ears. Compo body. Voice box. MARKS: ABG/1362/MADE IN GERMANY. 16" $150.00

Alt. Beck & Gottschalk: Bisque socket head. Open mouth. Sleep eyes. Compo. body baby. MARKS: ABG (in scroll)/1366. 14" $200.00

Alt. Beck & Gottschalk: Bisque head. Open mouth. Sleep eyes. Pierced ears. Compo. body. Baby. MARKS: ABG (in scroll)/1376/40. 16" $185.00

Alt. Beck & Gottschalk: Bisque socket head. Open mouth. Sleep eyes. Pierced ears. Compo. body baby. MARKS: ABG (in scroll)/1367/40/ MADE IN GERMANY 18" $200.00

Alt. Beck & Gottschalk: Bisque head with flange neck. Open mouth/ 2 lower teeth. Molded hair, sleep eyes & dimples. Cloth body. Compo. arms & legs. MARKS: COPR. BY GEORGENE AVERILL/1005/3652 /GERMANY/1386/30. 20" $650.00

Armand Marseille: Bisque socket head. Closed mouth. Sleep eyes. Compo. body lady doll. MARKS: GERMANY/M.H./A 30 M. 20" $285.00

Armand Marseille: Bisque head. Closed mouth. Sleep eyes. Pouty type. MARKS: G. 251 B./DRGM 243/1/A 2/0 M GERMANY. 16" $380.00

Armand Marseille: Bisque closed dome head. Closed mouth. Painted eyes. Molded hair to a point. Googlie. MARKS: GB 252 GERMANY/ A6/0 M DRGM 10" $475.00

Armand Marseille: Bisque head (socket). Compo. body. Bent leg baby. MARKS: MADE IN GERMANY/A O M 259/DRGM 16" $125.00

Armand Marseille. Painted bisque socket head. Closed mouth. Sleep eyes. Googlie girl. Compo. body. MARKS: JUST ME/REGISTERED /GERMAN/A 310 3/0 M. 12" $125.00

Armand Marseilles: For Geo. Borgfeldt & Co. Bisque closed dome head. Open mouth. Inset eyes. Paint hair. Comp. body. Bent limbs. Baby. MARKS: G328B A. M./GERMANY. 12" $125.00

Armand Marseilles: (1865-1928) Brown bisque closed dome head. Sleep eyes. Molded hair. Cloth body & joints. Celluloid hands. Baby. MARKS: A.M. 341/GERMANY. 7" $100.00

Armand Marseille: Bisque shoulder head. Open mouth. Stuffed canvas body. Bisque fore-arms. MARKS: 370/A.M. 0½ DEP/Armand Marseille/Made in Germany. 22" $140.00

Armand Marseille: Bisque shoulder head. Oilcloth body stuffed with hair. MARKS: 370/A.M. 4/OX DEP/Made in Germany. 17" $100.00

Armand Marseille: Bisque shoulder head. Open mouth. Sleep eyes. Kid body. Bisque fore-arms. Stuffed legs. MARKS: 370/A. M. 5/OX. 8" $65.00

Armand Marseille: Bisque shoulder head. Open mouth. Inset eyes. Wig. Dimpled chin. Kid body. MARKS: A. M. 380 2½ DEP/GERMANY. 18" $125.00

Armand Marseilles: Bisque socket head. Open mouth. Sleep eyes. Molded brows. Mache body. Wooden arms & legs. MARKS: Armand Marseille/390n A 6/0 M/DRGM 216. 16" $185.00

Armand Marseilles: Bisque socket head. Open closed mouth. Sleep eyes. Compo body marked "Jutta". MARKS: Armand Marseille/Germany/390/A 11/0 M. 16" $145.00

Armand Marseilles: Bisque socket head. Closed mouth. Sleep eyes. Compo body. Adult body. Character face. MARKS: Armand Marseille/Germany/401/A 5/0 M. 13" $675.00

Armand Marseilles: Bisque head. Molded hair. Compo body. Paint shoes. MARKS: A. M. 500 DRGM/GERMANY. 12" $200.00

Armand Marseilles: Bisque socket head. Closed mouth. Inset eyes. Character face. Compo body. MARKS: Germany/550/A 3 M/DRGM. 22" $365.00

Armand Marseilles: Bisque socket head. Open closed mouth. Inset eyes. Dimpled chin. Bent limbs. Boy. Girl. or Baby. MARKS: 590/A 5 M/GERMANY/DRGM. 10" $295.00

Armand Marseilles: Bisque shoulder head. Closed mouth. Paint eyes. Molded hair on C-dome. Dimples. May have bisque, cloth, or kid body. MARKS: 600 A 30 M/DRGM Germany. 12" $180.00

Armand Marseilles: Bisque head. Open mouth. Inset eyes. Compo body. Bent limbs. Baby. MARKS: A.M./917/Germany. 13" $145.00

Armand Marseilles: Bisque shoulder head. Open mouth. Inset eyes. Kid body. Bisque fore-arms. MARKS: A M 957 DEP. 16" $140.00

Armand Marseilles: Bisculoid socket head. Open mouth. Sleep eyes. Compo body. MARKS: A M/966 6/Made in Germany. 14" $95.00

Armand Marseilles: Bisque socket head. Open mouth. Sleep eyes. Voice box. Compo body. Baby. MARKS: Germany/971/A 5 M/D-RGM 267/1. 14" $145.00

Armand Marseilles: 1914. Bisque socket head. Open mouth. Inset eyes. Fat cheeks. 2 teeth. Character face. Compo baby body. MARKS: Armand Marseille/A 975 M/Germany. 16" $135.00

Armand Marseilles: Mechanical. Bisque socket head. Open mouth. Flirty eyes. Head and eyes move from side-to-side & tongue vibrates. Compo body. MARKS: A 980 M 16/Germany. 23" $375.00

Armand Marseilles: 1914. Tan bisque socket head. Open mouth. 2 teeth. Quiver tongue. Inset eyes. Tan compo body. Baby. MARKS: Germany/980 A 2 M/DRGM. 15" $150.00

Armand Marseilles: 1914. Bisque socket head. Dimples. Open mouth. 2 teeth. Tongue. Sleep eyes. Compo body. Baby. MARKS: Germany /A 985 M/ 8/0. 16" $160.00

Armand Marseilles: Bisque socket head. Open mouth. Sleep eyes. Toddler body. MARKS: Armand Marseille/Germany/991/A M. 14" $165.00

Armand Marseilles: Bisque shoulder head. Open mouth. Flirty sleep eyes. Kid body. Bisque forearms. MARKS: Germany/991/Kiddie Joy /A 8 M. 12" $165.00

Armand Marseilles: Bisque socket head. Dimples. Open mouth. 2 teeth. Sleep eyes. Compo body. Baby. MARKS: Armand Marseille/Germany /992/A 2/0 M. 12" $145.00

Armand Marseilles: For Seyfarth & Reinhardt (1906-1934) in 1923. Bisque socket head. Dimples. Open mouth. 2 teeth. Flirty sleep eyes. Mohair. Compo body. 4 joints. MARKS: Armand Marseille/995 2/ SuR in Sunburst/Germany. 16" $155.00

Armand Marseilles: Bisque socket head. Open closed mouth. 2 teeth. Sleep eyes. Compo body. Pierced nostrils. Baby. MARKS: Armand Marseille/Germany/996/A 4 M. 16" $165.00

ARMAND MARSEILLE

16" Socket head on 5 piece composition baby body. Cryer in back. Open mouth/2 upper teeth. MARKS: A.B.G./1361/40/MADE IN GERMANY/12. $165.00

ARMAND MARSEILLE

12" Socket head on mache & compo. "stick" body. Open mouth. MARKS: 310. This is the same mold no. as used for "Just Me". $75.00

ARMAND MARSEILLE

13" Socket head on fully jointed composition body. Sleep googly eyes. Closed mouth. MARKS: GERMANY/323/A 4/0 M. $550.00

ARMAND MARSEILLE

8" Socket head on crude stick type body. Intaglio eyes. Molded -painted hair. MARKS: 324/A 11 /0 M/GERMANY. $295.00

Armand Marseilles: Bisque shoulder head. Open mouth. 4 teeth. Sleep eyes. Cloth body. Compo arms & legs. MARKS: 997/Germany/Kiddie Joy/A 3 M. 14" $185.00

Armand Marseilles: Bisque head. Fur eyebrows. Kid body. Full joints. MARKS: 1374 Florodora/A G M/DRGM 374830. 23" $175.00

Armand Marseilles: Bisque head. Sleep eyes. Compo body. MARKS: 1894/A.M. 1½ DEP/Made in Germany. 16" $115.00

Armand Marseilles: Bisque socket head. Open mouth. Inset eyes. Kid body. Bisque forearms. Stuffed legs. MARKS: 1984 A.M./8/0 DEP/ Made in Germany. 14" $100.00

Armand Marseilles: Bisque socket head. Open mouth. Inset eyes. Kid body. Bisque forearms. MARKS: Made in Germany/Baby Betty in circle/DRGM. 20" $185.00

Armand Marseilles: Bisque c-dome head. Closed mouth. Painted eyes. Molded hair to a point knot. Side glance eyes. Compo body. Baby. Character face. MARKS: GB/A. M. 3 -04. 25" $210.00

Armand Marseilles: Bisque socket head. Open mouth. Sleep eyes. HH eye brows. Kid body. Bisque forearms. MARKS: Made in Germany /Florodora A 4 M. 20" $160.00

Armand Marseilles: Red bisque head. Open mouth. Inset eyes. Frowning character face. 2 holes over each ear. Compo body. MARKS: A.M./x Germany/4/0. 12" $185.00

Bahr & Proschild: Bisque socket. Open mouth. Sleep eyes. Molded eyebrows. Mache body. Baby. MARKS: BP in heart/585 13/Germany. 14" $245.00

Bahr & Proschild: Bisque socket head. Open closed mouth. Sleep eyes. Wig. Molded eyebrows. Compo body. No elbows. Toddler. MARKS: B&P between crossed sheilds/604/Germany. 16" $265.00

Bahr & Proschild: Bisque head. Open closed mouth. Tongue. Sleep eyes. Wig. Molded eyebrows. Compo body. MARKS: BP in heart/ 678. 16" $245.00

Bahr & Proschild: Bisque socket head. Open mouth. Inset eyes. Compo baby body. MARKS: 585 BP in heart 6/Made in Germany. 20" $300.00

Bahr & Proschild: Bisque socket head. Open mouth. 4 teeth. Sleep eyes. Compo body. Toddler. MARKS: BP in heart/535 G/Germany. 16" $265.00

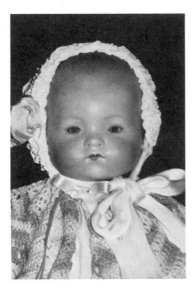

ARMAND MARSEILLE

12" DREAM BABY. 5 piece composition baby body. Sleep eyes.
Closed mouth. MARKS: A.M. 341
/10 OK. $125.00

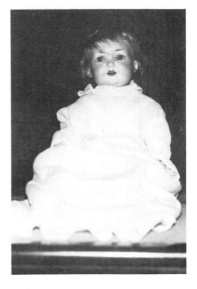

ARMAND MARSEILLE

13" Socket head. 5 piece composition bend leg baby body. Open
mouth. Sleep eyes. MARKS: GER-
MANY/971/A M/DRGM 26 7/8.
$145.00

ARMAND MARSEILLE

19" Socket head on composition,
fully jointed toddler body. MA-
RKS: A M/KOPPELSDORF/GER-
MANY/1330/A 9 M. $185.00

ARMAND MARSEILLE

28" Socket head on fully jointed
composition body. Open mouth.
Set brown eyes. MARKS: QUEEN
LOUISE/GERMANY/V $200.00

Bahr & Proschild: Bisque socket head. Open mouth. 2 teeth. Inset eyes. Molded hair. Compo body. Baby. MARKS: B&P in crossed swords 0/619/5/Germany. 14" $225.00

Bahr & Proschild: Bisque socket head. Open closed mouth. Felt tongue. 2 teeth. Dimples. Sleep eyes. Compo body. Baby. MARKS: B&P in crossed swords 0/624/8/Germany. 14" $235.00

Bahr & Proschild: Bisque socket head. Open mouth. 2 teeth. Quiver tongue. Flirty sleep eyes. Compo body. MARKS: 678 4/BP in heart /Made in Germany. 14" $245.00

Dressel, Cuno & Otto: Bisque head. Closed mouth. Sleep eyes. Compo body. MARKS: C&O Dressel Germany/2. 14" $365.00

Dressel, Cuno & Otto: Bisque shoulder head. Open mouth. Sleep eyes. Kid body. MARKS: C & O Dressel/93-8/0/Margaret Germany. 16" $165.00

Dressel, Cuno & Otto: Bisque head. Kid body. Sleep eyes. Open mouth. Pierced ears. MARKS: C O D 930/DEP. 14" $165.00

Dressel, Cuno & Otto: Bisque socket head. Closed mouth. Sleep eyes. Wig. Compo body. MARKS: 1469/C & O Dressel/Germany. 23" $225.00

CO Dressel by Armand Marseille: Bisque shoulder head. Chin dimple. Open mouth. 4 teeth. Inset eyes. Kid body. Bisque forearms. MARKS: 3/0/A 1776 M/COD N DEP/Made in Germany. 21" $185.00

CO Dressel by Armand Marseille: Bisque shoulder head. Open mouth. 4 teeth. Dimpled chin. Inset eyes. Kid body. Bisque forearms. MARKS: 1896/AM 12/0 DEP/Made in Germany. 21" $165.00

Dressel, Cuno & Otto: Bisque socket head. Open mouth. Sleep eyes. Teeth. Floating tongue. Character face. Compo body. MARKS: 1920 8/Jutta/Dressel. 16" $225.00

Dressel, Cuno & Otto: Bisque shoulder head. Open mouth. Inset eyes. Kid body. Bisque forearms. MARKS: COD 93 6 DEP. 12" $100.00

Handwerck, Max: Bisque socket head. Open mouth. 4 teeth. Sleep eyes. Compo body. MARKS: 23" $150.00

Handwerck, Max: 1910. Bisque socket head. Open mouth. 4 teeth. Sleep eyes. (21" - 125) Compo body. MARKS: 21" $135.00

Handwerck, Max: 1910. Bisque socket head. Open mouth. 4 teeth. Inset eyes. Compo body. MARKS: 16" $125.00

Handwerck, Heinrich: Bisque socket head. Open mouth. Sleep eyes. Pierced ears. Wooden body. MARKS: Germany/H. Handwerck/SIMON -HALBIG/6½. 16" $135.00

Handwerck, Heinrich: Body marked: Heinrich Handwerck. Bisque socket head. Open closed mouth. Inset eyes. Pierced ears. Compo body. MARKS: Handwerck 7/Germany. 20" $165.00

Handwerck, Heinrich: Body marked: Bebe Cosmopolite. 1895. Bisque socket head. Open mouth. Sleep eyes. Pierced ears. Smile, chin dimple. Wood body. MARKS: Heinrich Handwerck/SIMON-HALBIG/7. 22" $225.00

Handwerck, Heinrich: Trade name "Cherie". Bisque socket head. Closed mouth. Sleep eyes. Chin dimple. Compo body. MARKS: Heinrich Handwerck/SIMON-HALBIG/7½. 16" $595.00

Handwerck, Heinrich: Bisque head. Open mouth. Sleep eyes. Pierced ears. Compo body. MARKS: 69 12x/Germany/Handwerck/4. 18" $165.00

Handwerck, Heinrich: Bisque socket head. Open mouth. Inset eyes. Pierced ears. Compo body. MARKS: Heinrich Handwerck/SIMON-HALBIG/6. 18" $145.00

Handwerck, Heinrich: Bisque socket head. Open mouth. Sleep eyes. Chin dimple. 4 teeth. Pierced ears. Compo body. MARKS: 79 13/Handwerck/5/Germany. 14" $130.00

Handwerck, Heinrich: Bisque socket head. Open mouth. Sleep eyes. Compo body. MARKS: Germany/79 10 Handwerck 9. 20" $165.00

Handwerck, Heinrich: 1899. Bisque socket head. Pierced ears. Open mouth. 4 teeth. Sleep eyes. Compo body. MARKS: Germany/79 11 N/Handwerck. 28" $200.00

Handwerck, Heinrich: Bisque socket head. Open mouth. Sleep eyes. pierced ears. Compo body. MARKS: 79 10 Handwerck 9/Germany. 12" $115.00

Handwerck, Heinrich: Bisque socket head. Open mouth. Sleep eyes. Tongue. Pierced ears. Compo baby body. MARKS: 11½/99DEP Germany/HANDWERCK. 30" $285.00

Handwerck, Heinrich: 1899. Bisque socket head. Pierced ears. Open mouth. 4 teeth. Sleep eyes. Hair lashes. Compo body. MARKS: 99 16/HANDWERCK/DEP/Germany 7. 21" $165.00

Handwerck, Heinrich: Bisque socket head. Pierced ears. Open mouth. Sleep eyes. Compo body. MARKS: 11½ 99 DEP/HANDWERCK/HALBIG/Germany. 22" $170.00

Handwerck, Max: 1901. Bisque Socket head. Open mouth. Sleep eyes. Tongue. Character. Compo body. Baby. MARKS: Max Handwerck /Bebe Elite/B 90 185/Germany 3. 18" $325.00

Handwerck, Max: Bisque socket head. Open mouth. Sleep eyes. Compo body. MARKS: 21" $135.00

Handwerck, Max: 1910. Bisque socket head. Open mouth. Sleep eyes. Turns head when walking. Compo body. No knee joint. MARKS: 18" $165.00

Handwerck, Max: 1910. Bisque socket head. Open mouth. Sleep eyes. Compo body. MARKS: 18" $145.00

Handwerck, Max: 1910. Bisque socket head. Open mouth. 4 teeth. Sleep eyes. Compo body. MARKS: 16" $125.00

Handwerck, Max: Bisque shoulder head. Open mouth. Sleep eyes. Kid body. Celluloid hands. Made in 1910. MARKS: 14" $100.00

Handwerck, Max: Bisque socket head. Open mouth. Inset eyes. Compo body. MARKS: Max Handwerck/283 307/Germany. 21" $225.00

Handwerck, Max: 1901. Bisque socket head. Open mouth. Sleep eyes. Head was made by William Goebel. Compo baby body. MARKS: Max Handwerck/Bebe Elite/286 3/Germany. 18" $325.00

Handwerck, Max: Bisque socket head. Open mouth. Sleep eyes. Compo body. MARKS: 287 H 0½. 18" $245.00

Handwerck, Max: Bisque socket head. Open mouth. Inset eyes. Compo body. MARKS: Handwerck/Germany 3x/2½. 18" $195.00

Handwerck, Heinrich: Bisque socket head. Open mouth. 4 teeth. Pierced ears. Sleep eyes. Compo body. MARKS: N/DEP/Germany/ Handwerck/0½. 18" $145.00

Handwerck, Heinrich: Bisque socket head. Open mouth. Inset eyes. Pierced ears. Compo body. MARKS: Heinrich Handwerck/SIMON -HALBIG/6. 18" $165.00

Handwerck, Heinrich: 1893. Bisque socket head. Open mouth. 4 teeth. Chin dimple. Pierced ears. Inset eyes. Compo body. MARKS: Heinrich /Handwerck/SIMON-HALBIG/7/ (body) Bebe Cosmopolite. 18" $175.00

Handwerck, Heinrich: Bisque socket head. Open mouth. Sleep eyes. Compo body. MARKS: Handwerck/Germany/6½. 14" $135.00

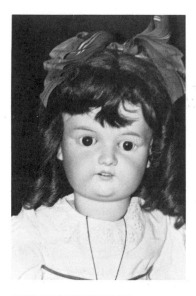

ARMAND MARSEILLE

32" Socket head. Fully jointed composition body. Open mouth. Molded brows. MARKS: A 17 M. $285.00

BAHR & PROSCHILD

12" Socket head on composition toddler body. Open/closed mouth with painted teeth. MARKS: B P, in crossed swords/585. $245.00

DRESSEL, CUNO & OTTO

8" Shoulder head on kid body with bisque forearms. Open mouth. MARKS: Holz Masse (see index) $85.00

DRESSEL, CUNO & OTTO

12" Shoulder head on kid body with bisque forearms. Open mouth. Unpierced ears. MARKS: LILLY /15/0. $75.00

Handwerck, Heinrich: Bisque socket head. Pierced ears. Chin dimple. Open mouth. 4 teeth. Sleep eyes. Compo walking body. MARKS: 11½ 99 DEP/Germany. 22" $170.00

Handwerck, Heinrich: 1899. Bisque socket head. Pierced. Open mouth. 4 teeth. Sleep eyes. Compo body. Voice box with string. MARKS: 11½ 99 DEP/Germany H 3. 23" $195.00

Handwerck, Heinrich: Bisque socket head. Pierced ears. Compo body. MARKS: 99 11 3/4 DEP/Handwerck Germany. 16" $145.00

Handwerck, Heinrich: Bisque socket head. Open mouth. Sleep eyes. Pierced ears. Compo body. MARKS: 99 16 Handwerck. 26" $185.00

Handwerck, Heinrich: Bisque socket head. Pierced ears. Open mouth. 4 teeth. Sleep eyes. Compo body. MARKS: 14 99 DEP/Handwerck 5½/Germany. 14" $125.00

Handwerck, Heinrich: Bisque socket head. Open mouth. Sleep eyes. Wig. Compo baby body. MARKS: 99 7/Germany. 16" $165.00

Handwerck, Heinrich: Bisque socket head. Open mouth. Sleep eyes. Pierced ears. Compo body. MARKS: 14 99 DEP/(body) Handwerck. 16" $145.00

Handwerck, Heinrich: Bisque socket head. Open mouth. Sleep eyes. Pierced ears. Hair lashes. Compo body. MARKS: 99 16 Handwerck /DEP Germany. 28" $190.00

Handwerck, Heinrich: 1899. Bisque socket head. Pierced ears. Open mouth. 4 teeth. Compo body. MARKS: 100 15 DEP/HANDWERCK /GERMANY. 30" $225.00

Handwerck, Heinrich: Bisque socket head. Open mouth. Sleep eyes. Compo body. MARKS: HANDWERCK/109 11/Germany/2½. 18" $165.00

Handwerck, Heinrich: Bisque socket head. Open mouth. Inset eyes. Pierced ears. Compo body marked; Handwerck. MARKS: HAND-WERCK (body)/109 12 (head)/Germany. 23" $185.00

Handwerck, Heinrich: 1900. Bisque socket head. Closed mouth. Inset eyes. HH. Compo body. MARKS: HANDWERCK/109 11½. 18" $495.00

Handwerck, Heinrich: 1899. Bisque socket head. Pierced ears. Chin dimple. Open mouth. 4 teeth. Sleep eyes. Compo body. MARKS: 109 7½/Germany/HANDWERCK. 14" $145.00

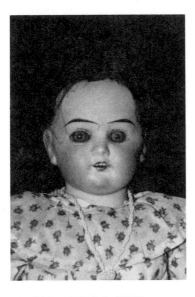

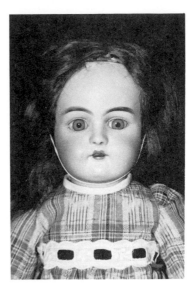

DRESSEL, CUNO & OTTO

16" Shoulder head on kid body with bisque forearms. Open mouth. Unpierced ears. Original dress. MARKS: Holz Masse mark (see index)/90.

HEINRICH HANDWERCK

18" Socket head on fully jointed composition body. Open mouth. Sleep eyes. MARKS: HAND-WERCK 79-10. $160.00

HEINRICH HANDWERCK

21" Socket head on fully jointed composition body. Open mouth. MARKS: 109-7½. $175.00

HEINRICH HANDWERCK

22" Shoulder head. Kid body with bisque lower arms. Applied ears. Open mouth. MARKS: X, high on crown. HcH 2 H. $165.00

Handwerck, Heinrich: 1899. Bisque socket head. Pierced ears. Chin dimple. Open mouth. 4 teeth. Sleep eyes. Compo body. MARKS: 109 11 3/4/Germany/HANDWERCK (body). 22" $180.00

Handwerck, Heinrich: 1899. Bisque socket head. Pierced ears. Chin dimple. Open mouth. 2 teeth. Inset eyes. Compo body. MARKS: 109 12 N DEP/Germany/HANDWERCK 4. 16" $145.00

Handwerck, Heinrich: 1899. Bisque socket head. Pierced ears. Open mouth. 3 teeth. Chin dimple. Sleep eyes. Compo body. MARKS: 109 12 N DEP/Germany/HANDWERCK 4½. 30" $225.00

Handwerck, Heinrich: 1899. Bisque socket head. Pierced ears. Dimpled chin. Open mouth. 4 teeth. Inset eyes. Compo body. MARKS: 109 16 DEP/Germany/HANDWERCK 16 (body). 36" $300.00

Handwerck, Heinrich: 1899. Bisque socket head. Pierced ears. Dimpled chin. Open mouth. 4 teeth. Compo body. MARKS: 109 15½ DEP/ Germany/HANDWERCK 6½. 32" $290.00

Handwerck, Heinrich: 1899. Bisque socket head. Pierced ears. Open mouth. 4 teeth. Sleep eyes. Compo body. MARKS: 119 3 DEP/HAND-WERCK/Germany 5. 18" $240.00

Handwerck, Heinrich: Bisque socket head. Open mouth. Inset eyes. Pierced ears. 2 holes in back of head. Compo body. MARKS: Hand-werck 5/119. 23" $265.00

Handwerck, Heinrich: Bisque socket head. 2 holes in back of head. Pierced ears. Compo body. MARKS: HANDWERCK 5/119. 16" $225.00

Handwerck, Heinrich: Bisque socket head. Pierced ears. 2 holes in back of head. Compo body. MARKS: HANDWERCK 5 HALBIG/ 119 13. 12" $185.00

Handwerck, Heinrich: Bisque socket head. Open mouth. Inset eyes. Pierced ears. 2 holes in back of head. Compo body. MARKS: 119 13/Handwerck 5/HALBIG. 30" $315.00

Handwerck, Heinrich: 1899. Bisque socket head. Pierced ears. Open mouth. 4 teeth. Sleep eyes. Compo body. MARKS: 119 10 DEP/ HANDWERCK/Germany 4. 36" $345.00

Handwerck, Heinrich: Marked: Bebe Cosmopolite. 1895. Bisque socket head. Open mouth. Sleep eyes. Pierced ears. Dimpled chin. Wood body. MARKS: Heinrich Handwerck/SIMON-HALBIG 7/(body) 1290 124 7. 18" $285.00

Handwerck, Heinrich: 1899. Bisque socket head. Pierced ears. Open mouth. 4 teeth. Sleep eyes. Compo body. MARKS: 199-10/4/HAND-WERCK/Germany. 22" $210.00

Handwerck, Heinrich: Bisque head. Cotton filled kid body. Bisque forearms. MARKS: Made in Germany/Hch (Horseshoe) H/O. 16" $125.00

Handwerck, Heinrich: 1887. Bisque shoulder head. Closed mouth. Inset eyes. Cotton filled Kid body. Bisque forearms. MARKS: Hch (horseshoe) 3. 18" $135.00

Handwerck, Heinrich: Bisque shoulder head. Open closed mouth. Inset eyes. Kid body. Cloth fore-legs. Bisque forearms. MARKS: Hch 3/0 H/Germany. 22" $165.00

Handwerck, Heinrich: Bisque head. Open mouth. Sleep eyes. Kid body. Bisque forearms. MARKS: (horseshoe)/Hch 5/0 H. 25" $185.00

Heubach, Gebruder: Bisque socket head. Closed mouth. Googlie paint eyes. Molded hair. Compo body. MARKS: 5D/58 90 Heubach (in square)/Germany. 12" $385.00

Heubach, Gebruder: Bisque socket head. Hair molded. Closed dome. Molded hair bow. Closed mouth. Painted eyes. Compo body. MARKS: 5 85 Heubach (in square) 58/Germany. 16" $325.00

Heubach, Gebruder: Bisque socket head. Hair molded. Closed dome. Painted eyes. Open mouth. Googlie. MARKS: 5D/58 90 Heubach (in square) 56/Germany. 9" $500.00

Heubach, Gebruder: Bisque head. Open closed mouth. Sleep eyes. Tongue. Teeth rest on tongue. Hair eyeslashes. Compo body. Bent limbs. MARKS: 9/Heubach (in square)/Germany. 20" $365.00

Heubach, Gebruder: Bisque socket & plate head. Open closed mouth. Painted eyes. Blonde molded hair. Cloth body. Bisque forearms & legs. MARKS: Heubach (in square)/Germany 6. 18" $280.00

Heubach, Gebruder: Bisque socket head. Open closed mouth. 2 teeth. Painted eyes. Smile. Compo body. MARKS: 14" $300.00

Heubach, Gebruder: Bisque socket head. Molded curls. Closed dome. Open closed mouth. Painted eyes. MARKS: 5D/87 Heubach (in square) 99/Germany. 12" $265.00

Heubach, Gebruder: Bisque head. Flanged neck. Closed dome. Open closed mouth. Painted eyes. Molded blonde hair. Cloth straw-stuffed body. Compo. Pink felt upper legs. MARKS: 8 Heubach (in square) 14/Germany. 16" $200.00

Heubach, Gebruder: Bisque socket head. Open closed mouth. 6 teeth. Painted eyes. Molded blonde. Compo body. MARKS: 8 Heubach (in square) 68/Germany. 16" $450.00

Heubach, Gebruder: Bisque shoulder head. Hair molded. Closed dome. Closed mouth. Character face. Cloth body. MARKS: 17 Heubach (in square) 24/Germany. 18" $385.00

Heubach, Gebruder: Bisque head. Closed dome. Closed mouth. Molded curls. Compo body. MARKS: 30 95 Heubach (in square) 11 94/Germany 6/0. 9" $185.00

Heubach, Gebruder: Bisque head. Closed dome. Blonde hair molded close. Closed mouth. Painted eyes. Compo body. MARKS: 35 Heubach (in square) 91/Germany. 16" $285.00

Heubach, Gebruder: Bisque socket head. Closed mouth. Googlie. Mache body. Sleep eyes. MARKS: Elizabeth 6/0/Heubach Germany. 9" $500.00

Heubach, Gebruder: Bisque socket head. Open mouth. Sleep eyes. Compo body. Joints above formed knees. MARKS: Heubach (in square)/G 2 H. 12" $365.00

Heubach, Gebruder: Googlie. Bisque socket head. Closed watermelon mouth. Flirty sleep eyes. Smile. Compo body. Voice box. MARKS: 2/0/Heubach (in square)/Germany. 12" $750.00

Heubach, Gebruder: Bisque socket head. Open closed mouth with teeth showing. Flirty paint eyes. Smile. Compo body. Bent limbs. MARKS: 0/Heubach (in square)/Germany. 16" $400.00

Heubach, Gebruder: Bisque shoulder head. Closed mouth. Painted eyes. Molded blonde hair. Kid body. Bisque forearms. MARKS: Heubach (in square)/2 Germany/101. 14" $425.00

Heubach, Gebruder: Bisque socket head. Closed mouth. Painted eyes. Molded hair. Compo body. MARKS: 1 76 Heubach (in square) 02/Germany. 12" $265.00

Heubach, Gebruder: Bisque socket head. Closed mouth. Closed dome. Paint eyes. Molded hair. Googlie. Smile. Compo body. Bent limbs. MARKS: 9/Heubach (in square)/Germany. 9" $675.00

Heubach, Gebruder: Bisque socket head. Closed dome. Closed mouth. Molded curls. Compo body. MARKS: 4 12 Heubach (in square) 02/Germany. 12" $300.00

Heubach, Gebruder: "Whistling Jim". Bisque socket head. Closed dome. Open mouth. Painted eyes. Molded hair. Character face. Stuffed pink cloth body. Compo hands. Squeeze for music. MARKS: Germany /3/Heubach (in square)/37 74. 14" $650.00

Heubach, Gebruder: Bisque socket head. Molded hair. Closed dome. Closed mouth. Painted eyes. Compo body. MARKS: 4 83 Heubach (in square) 81. 12" $285.00

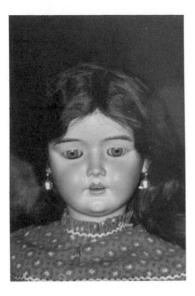

HEUBACH, G.

42" Socket head on fully jointed composition body. Open mouth. Pierced ears. Sleep eyes. MARKS: HANDWERCK. $365.00

HEUBACH, G.

15" Socket head on composition body. Molded-painted hair. Open closed mouth with 4 upper & 2 lower painted teeth. MARKS: 3/ HEUBACH, in square. $450.00

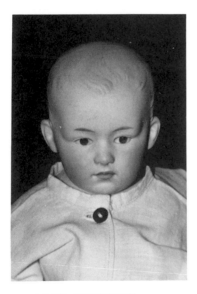

HEUBACH, GEBRUDER

14" Socket head on fully jointed composition body. Painted eyes. Closed mouth. MARKS: 3/GER-MANY $265.00

HEUBACH, GEBRUDER

26" Socket head on fully jointed composition body. Open mouth. MARKS: 30.7/GBR 165 H/10/ GERMANY. $225.00

Heubach, Gebruder: Bisque shoulder head. Closed dome. Closed mouth. Painted eyes. Molded blonde hair ribbon. Head turned to one side. Kid body. Bisque forearms. Cloth fore-legs. MARKS: 78 Heubach (in square) 56/1 Germany. 20" $395.00

Heubach, Gebruder: Bisque head. Compo body. MARKS: 82 Heubach (in square) 32/Germany 8/0. 23" $295.00

Heubach, Gebruder: Bisque head. Closed dome. Open closed mouth. Painted eyes. Side glance. Molded hair. Compo body. MARKS: Heubach (in square)/87 HU 29. 12" $450.00

Heubach, Gebruder: Bisque socket head. Closed dome. Closed mouth. Painted eyes. One eye winks. Molded blonde hair. Compo body. MARKS: Germany/91 Heubach (in square) 41. 12" $380.00

Heubach, Gebruder: Bisque socket head. Sleep eyes. 2 holes over each ear. Googlie. Mache body. MARKS: 95 Heubach (in square) 75/Germany 5/0. 12" $475.00

Heubach, Gebruder: Bisque shoulder head. Open closed mouth. Sleep eyes. Calico stuffed body. Gusseted knees. Compo arms. MARKS: HEUBACH/275 6/0. 16" $195.00

Heubach, Gebruder: Bisque boy in one piece, sitting on an egg. Wears a hat with pink lined rabbit ears. Open mouth. Painted eyes. Hair molded. MARKS: HEUBACH/96643. 6" $280.00

Heubach, Gebruder: Bisque socket head. Closed mouth. Sleep eyes. 2 holes behind each ear. Compo body. Googlie. MARKS: 10542 4/0/ Heubach Germany. 12" $395.00

Heubach, Gebruder: Bisque head. Kid body. MARKS: 10633/Heubach Germany. 16" $265.00

Heubach, Gebruder: Bisque socket head. Closed mouth. Sleep eyes. Long pouty. Compo body. MARKS: Germany/heubach (in square) /42. 18" $225.00

Heubach, Gebruder: Bisque socket head. Closed mouth. Painted eyes. Molded hair. Compo body. MARKS: 0716/Heubach (in square)/ Germany. 15" $395.00

Heubach, Gebruder: Bisque socket head. Closed mouth. Painted eyes. Molded hair. Character face. Compo body. MARKS: 0746/Heubach (in square)/Germany. 16" $400.00

Heubach, Gebruder: Bisque socket head. Open mouth. 2 teeth. Sleep eyes. Compo body. Bent limbs. MARKS: 12/Heubach (in square)/ 750/Germany. 16" $325.00

HEUBACH, G.

17" Socket head on fully jointed toddler body. Sleep eyes. Closed mouth. MARKS: 5/GERMANY/ HEUBACH, in square. $280.00

HEUBACH, G.

10" Socket head on 5 piece bent leg baby body. Closed mouth. Sleep eyes. MARKS: 6929/GERMANY/ 2/HEUBACH, in square. $215.00

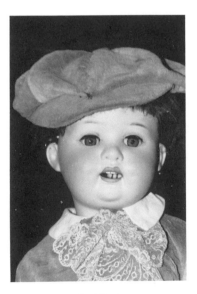

HEUBACH, KOPPELSDORF

20" Socket head with 5 piece composition body. Open mouth (tongue gone). MARKS: HEU-BACH KOPPELSDORF/300-7. $165.00

HEUBACH KOPPELSDORF

22" Shoulder head on kid body with bisque forearms. Open mouth. MARKS: 1900-0. $165.00

Heubach, Gebruder: Bisque shoulder head. Closed mouth. Intaglo eyes. Painted closed dome. Pouty boy. Cloth body. MARKS: Heubach /6692 3/Germany. 12" $225.00

Heubach, Gebruder: Bisque shoulder head. Closed mouth. Painted eyes. Molded blonde hair. Baby. Pouty. Cloth body. MARKS: 6894/ Gebruder Heubach/86/Germany. 14" $245.00

Heubach, Gebruder: Bisque shoulder head. Dimples. Open mouth. Inset eyes. Molded hair. Kid body. Compo arms & legs. MARKS: HEUBACH/7054 45. 18" $225.00

Heubach, Gebruder: Bisque shoulder head. Closed mouth. Painted eyes. Molded blonde boy's hair. Kid body. Bisque forearms. MARKS: Heubach (in square)/7072 4/Germany. 22" $245.00

Heubach, Gebruder: Bisque socket head. Closed mouth. Sleep eyes. Compo body. MARKS: Germany/7246/Heubach (in square) 46 (ink). 14" $200.00

Heubach, Gebruder: Bisque shoulder head. Closed mouth. Inset eyes. Cloth body. Bisque forearms. MARKS: 7345/11/0/Heubach (in square) /Germany. 16" $325.00

Heubach, Gebruder: Bisque socket head. Googlie. Closed mouth. Painted eyes. Painted hair. Compo body. MARKS: 2/0/7602/30 Heubach (in square)/Germany. 9" $600.00

Heubach, Gebruder: Bisque socket head. Open closed mouth. 2 low teeth. Painted eyes. Molded blonde hair. Smile. Mache body. MARKS: Germany/Heubach (in square)/7604 DEP 5/0. 12" $400.00

Heubach, Gebruder: Bisque socket head. Open closed mouth. 2 low teeth. Painted eyes. Painted hair. Compo body. Bent limbs. Smile. MARKS: 7802/ Heubach (in square)/Germany. 12" $365.00

Heubach, Gebruder: Bisque shoulder head. Closed mouth. Painted eyes. Molded blonde hair with ribbon. Kid body. Bisque forearms. MARKS: 6/0 Germany/Heubach (in square)/7856. 14" $350.00

Heubach, Gebruder: Bisque socket head. Closed mouth. Painted eyes. Molded hair on closed dome. Character face. Compo body. MARKS: Germany/Heubach (in square)/8004. 12" $385.00

Heubach, Gebruder: Bisque shoulder head. Open mouth. Teeth. Sleep eyes. Kid body. Bisque forearms. MARKS: 8232 8/0/Heubach (in square)/Germany. 15" $295.00

Heubach (Ernst), Koppelsdorf: Bisque shoulder head. Open closed mouth. Sleep eyes. Calico body. Gusseted knees. Compo arms. MARKS: 11/Heubach/275 6/0. (called: Our Pet). 18" $145.00

Heubach (Ernst), Koppelsdorf: Bisque socket head. Open mouth. Sleep eyes. Compo body. Made for Seyfarth & Reinhardt. MARKS: Heubach-Koppelsdorf/312 SuR(in sunburst) 18. 18" $165.00

Heubach (Ernst), Koppelsdorf: Brown bisque socket head. Closed mouth. Inset eyes. Painted hair. Thick lips. Brown compo body. MARKS: Heubach-Koppelsdorf/99 616/Germany. 20" $155.00

Heubach (Ernst), Koppelsdorf: Bisque socket head. Open mouth. Sleep eyes. Spring-strung compo body. MARKS: Heubach-Koppelsdorf /230 3/Germany. 16" $135.00

Heubach (Ernst), Koppelsdorf: Bisque socket head. Open mouth. Sleep eyes. Belton-type head. Eye lashes. Mache body. MARKS: Heubach-Koppelsdorf/250 4 Germany. 20" $145.00

Heubach (Ernst), Koppelsdorf: Bisque head. Sleep eyes. Compo body. MARKS: Heubach-Koppelsdorf/250 S Germany. 23" $165.00

Heubach (Ernst), Koppelsdorf: 1900. Bisque socket head. Open mouth. Sleep eyes. Belton-type head. Mache body. MARKS: Heubach -Koppelsdorf/250 4 Germany. 26" $185.00

Heubach (Ernst), Koppelsdorf: 1900. Bisque socket head. Open mouth. Sleep eyes. Dimpled chin. Compo body. MARKS: Heubach -Koppelsdorf/25 - 6/Germany. 16" $145.00

Heubach (Ernst), Koppelsdorf: 1900. Bisque socket head. Open mouth. Sleep eyes. Compo body. MARKS: Heubach/250 6½/Koppelsdorf. 28" $195.00

Heubach (Ernst), Koppelsdorf: 1900. Bisque socket head. Dimpled chin. Open mouth. 4 teeth. Sleep eyes. Lamb's wool wig. Compo body. Stick legs. MARKS: Heubach-Koppelsdorf/250 4/Thuringia. 18" $145.00

Heubach (Ernst), Koppelsdorf: Bisque head and body with mache arms and legs. Open mouth. 3 teeth. Sleep eyes. MARKS: Heubach -Koppelsdorf/251 17/0/Germany. 16" $135.00

Heubach (Ernst), Koppelsdorf: Bisque socket head. Dimples. Open mouth. 2 teeth. Inset eyes. Compo body. Bent limbs. MARKS: Heubach-Koppelsdorf/267 6/Germany/DRGM. 18" $165.00

Heubach (Ernst), Koppelsdorf: Bisque socket head. Dimples. Open mouth. Sleep eyes. Mohair. Compo body. Toddler. MARKS: 267. 4. 7./E H/Germany. 20" $165.00

Heubach (Ernst), Koppelsdorf: Bisque shoulder head. Dimpled chin. Open mouth. Sleep eyes. Kid body. Bisque forearms. Cloth legs. MARKS: Germany/275 12/0. Our pet (body). 28" $165.00

Heubach (Ernst), Koppelsdorf: 1920. Bisque shoulder head. Dimpled chin. Open mouth. 4 teeth. Sleep eyes. Kidette body. Celluloid hands. MARKS: Heubach/275 13/0/Koppelsdorf-Germany. 12" $100.00

Heubach (Ernst), Koppelsdorf: 1920. Bisque socket head. Open mouth. 2 teeth. Quiver tongue. Sleep eyes. Compo body. Bent limbs. MARKS: Heubach-Koppelsdorf/300 9/0/Germany. 16" $135.00

Heubach (Ernst), Koppelsdorf: 1920. Bisque socket head of musical key wind doll. Dimples. Open mouth. 2 teeth. Quiver tongue. Sleep eyes. Compo body. Straight legs. MARKS: Heubach-Koppelsdorf /300 30 2/0/Germany. 26" $225.00

Heubach (Ernst), Koppelsdorf: Bisque socket head. Open mouth. Sleep eyes. Compo body. MARKS: Heubach-Koppelsdorf/12 Germany 302. 18" $165.00

Heubach (Ernst), Koppelsdorf: Bisque socket head. Open mouth. 4 teeth. Sleep eyes. Compo body. Wood upper arms & legs. MARKS: Heubach-Koppelsdorf/302 15/Germany. 23" $185.00

Heubach (Ernst), Koppelsdorf: Bisque head. Open mouth. Sleep eyes. Compo body. MARKS: Heubach-Koppelsdorf/312 Germany. 14" $125.00

Heubach (Ernst), Koppelsdorf: Bisque socket head. Open mouth. Sleep eyes. Compo body. MARKS: Heubach-Koppelsdorf/SuR (in sunburst) /312 2/Germany. 18" $145.00

Heubach (Ernst), Koppelsdorf: Bisque socket head. Open mouth. Sleep eyes. Tongue. Compo baby body. MARKS: Heubach-Koppelsdorf/ 317 3/0/Germany. 23" $165.00

Heubach (Ernst), Koppelsdorf: Bisque socket head. Open mouth. Sleep eyes. Pouty. Compo body. MARKS: Heubach-Koppelsdorf/320 Germany. 16" $165.00

Heubach (Ernst), Koppelsdorf: Bisque socket head. Open mouth. Sleep eyes. Googlie. Compo body. MARKS: Heubach-Koppelsdorf/320 8/0/Germany. 9" $395.00

Heubach (Ernst), Koppelsdorf: 1920. Bisque socket head. Dimpled chin. Open mouth. 2 teeth. Breather. Sleep eyes. Compo body. MARKS: Heubach-Koppelsdorf/320 40/Germany. 18" $185.00

Heubach (Ernst), Koppelsdorf: Bisque socket head. Open mouth. Sleep eyes. Compo body. MARKS: Heubach-Koppelsdorf/321 11/0/Germany. 16" $145.00

KAMMER & REINHARDT

7½" Socket head on 5 piece mache body with straight legs. Sleep eyes. Open mouth. MARKS: SIMON HALBIG/K star R/17. $85.00

KAMMER & REINHARDT
13" Socket head on full jointed composition body. Molded-painted hair. Sleep eyes. Open mouth with molded tongue and 2 upper teeth. MARKS: SIMON & HALBIG/K star R/26. $895.00

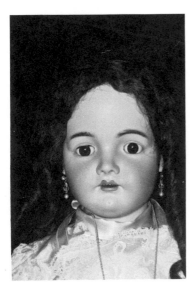

KAMMER & REINHARDT

40" Socket head on fully jointed composition & wood body. Molded brows. Sleep eyes. Open mouth. MARKS: W, on front of crown. S & H/K star R, on back of head. $350.00

KAMMER & REINHARDT

8" "PETER & MARIE" Socket heads on composition bodies. Closed pouty mouths. Painted eyes. MARKS: K star R/101. Both completely original. $800.00 each.

Heubach (Ernst), Koppelsdorf: Bisque socket head. Open closed mouth. Sleep eyes. Flirty character face. MARKS: Heubach-Koppelsdorf/342/2 Germany. 16" $285.00

Heubach (Ernst), Koppelsdorf: Bisque socket head. Open closed mouth. Sleep eyes. 2 teeth. Compo body. Stick legs. MARKS: Heubach-Koppelsdorf/342 1/9/0. 20" $315.00

Heubach (Ernst), Koppelsdorf: Bisque socket head. Dimpled chin. Open mouth. 2 teeth. Quiver tongue. Flirty sleep eyes. Breather. Compo body. Bent limbs. MARKS: Heubach-Koppelsdorf/342 5/ Germany. 16" $185.00

Heubach (Ernst), Koppelsdorf: Brown bisque socket head. Closed mouth. Inset eyes. Closed dome. Painted hair. Pierced ears. Compo body. Bent limbs. MARKS: Heubach-Koppelsdorf/399 16/0/Germany. 18" $250.00

Heubach (Ernst), Koppelsdorf: Brown bisque socket head. Pierced ears. Closed mouth. Full red lips. Sleep eyes. Painted hair. Brown compo body. MARKS: Heubach-Koppelsdorf/399 12/0/DRGM/Germany. Black Sambo (box). 12" $250.00

Heubach (Ernst), Koppelsdorf: Bisque socket head. Open mouth. Sleep eyes. 4 teeth. Character face. Compo body. MARKS: Heubach-Koppelsdorf/407 13/0a/Germany. 16" $225.00

Heubach (Ernst), Koppelsdorf: A black toddler. Brown bisque socket head. Open mouth. Sleep eyes. Compo body. MARKS: Heubach-Koppelsdorf/438/Germany. 16" $315.00

Heubach (Ernst), Koppelsdorf: Bisque head. Flanged neck. Open mouth. Sleep eyes. Molded black hair. Pierced ears. Head is tinted brown. Cloth body. Brown compo arms & legs. MARKS: Heubach-Koppelsdorf/450 4/0/DRGM Germany. (a black). 12" $185.00

Heubach (Ernst), Koppelsdorf: Brown bisque socket head. Pierced ears. Closed mouth. Inset eyes. Painted hair. Brown Compo body. MARKS: Heubach-Koppelsdorf/99 616/Germany. 16" $425.00

Heubach (Ernst), Koppelsdorf: Bisque socket head. Open mouth. Sleep eyes. Compo body. MARKS: Heubach-Koppelsdorf/2504/Germany. 10" $125.00

Heubach (Ernst), Koppelsdorf: Bisque socket head. Open mouth. Sleep eyes. Tongue. Compo body. Bent limbs. MARKS: Heubach-Koppelsdorf/3427. 12" $125.00

Heubach (Ernst), Koppelsdorf: Bisque socket head. Open mouth. Sleep eyes. Mache body. Bent baby limbs. MARKS: Heubach-Koppelsdorf /32144 Germany. 12" $135.00

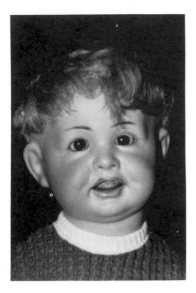

KAMMER & REINHARDT

12" Socket head on 5 piece baby body. Open mouth/tremble tongue & 2 upper teeth. Sleep eyes. MARKS: K star R/SIMON & HALBIG /116/A. $450.00

KAMMER & REINHARDT

16" Socket head on 5 piece bent leg baby body. Sleep eyes. Open mouth. MARKS: K star R/SIMON & HALBIG/126. $195.00

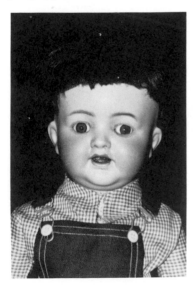

KAMMER & RINEHARDT

20" Socket head on toddler composition fully jointed body. Flirty, sleep eyes. Open mouth/2 upper teeth. MARKS: K star R/SIMON & HALBIG/126. $225.00

KESTNER, J.D.

23" Socket head on fully jointed composition body. Sleep eyes. Open mouth. Original clothes. MARKS: GERMANY/B 3/incised check mark. $185.00

Kammer & Reinhardt: Chocolate bisque socket head. Closed mouth. Sleep eyes. Pierced ears. Wood body. MARKS: SIMON HALBIG/K star R/53. 19" $450.00

Kammer & Reinhardt: 1900. Bisque socket head. Closed mouth. Compo body. MARKS: SIMON HALBIG/K star R/55. 12" $200.00

Kammer & Reinhardt: Bisque head. Open mouth. Sleep eyes. Kid body. MARKS: K star R 60. 18" $145.00

Kammer & Reinhardt: Celluloid shoulder head. Molded hair. Open mouth. Inset eyes. Cloth body. Excelsior stuffing. Compo arms & legs. MARKS: K star R/65/Turtlemark. 20" $165.00

Kammer & Reinhardt: 1896. Bisque shoulder head. Open mouth. 4 teeth. Sleep eyes. Kid body Bisque forearms. MARKS: K star R/Germany/70. 19" $145.00

Kammer & Reinhardt: 1896. Bisque socket head. Pierced ears. Open mouth. 4 teeth. Sleep eyes. Compo BJ body. MARKS: HALBIG/K star R/70. 22" $160.00

Kammer & Reinhardt: "The Flirt" made in 1908. Bisque socket head. Pierced ears. Open mouth. Flirty sleep eyes. Eyelids move with eyes. Compo body. MARKS: SIMON-HALBIG/K star R/Germany/68. 20" $325.00

Kammer & Reinhardt: Bisque socket head. Open mouth. Inset eyes. Character face. Compo body. MARKS: SIMON-HALBIG/K star R/73. 24" $200.00

Kammer & Reinhardt: 1905. Bisque socket head. Open mouth. Sleep eyes. Compo walking body. MARKS: SIMON-HALBIG/K star R/75. 24" $180.00

Kammer & Reinhardt: Bisque socket head. Open mouth. Pierced ears. Compo. Body. MARKS: K star R/SH 76. 28" $225.00

Kammer & Reinhardt: Bisque socket head. Open mouth. Sleep eyes. Pierced ears. Compo body. MARKS: SIMON-HALBIG/K star R/80. 32" $350.00

Kammer & Reinhardt: 1905. Bisque socket head. Pierced ears. Open mouth. 4 teeth. Sleep eyes. Compo BJ body. MARKS: SIMON-HALBIG/K star R/Germany/85. 19" $145.00

Kammer & Reinhardt: 1909. Bisque socket character head. Open closed mouth. Painted eyes. Molded hair. Pouty. Compo body. MARKS: K star R/100/28. 15" $600.00

43

Kammer & Reinhardt: Bisque socket head. Closed mouth. Pouty. Painted eyes. Flocked hair. Compo body. MARKS: K star R/100 X /48. 15" $600.00

Kammer & Reinhardt: 1897. Bisque socket head. Open mouth. Sleep eyes. Compo body. Painted socks and shoes. MARKS: HALBIG/K star R/15. 22" $160.00

Kammer & Reinhardt: 1897. Bisque socket head. Open mouth. 4 teeth. Sleep eyes. Compo body. Molded shoes. MARKS: HALBIG/K star R/Germany/17. 19" $145.00

Kammer & Reinhardt: 1920. Bisque socket head. Open mouth. Sleep eyes. Wig. Tongue. Smile. Character face. Compo body. Bent arms & legs. MARKS: K star R/S & H 126 20½. 20" $300.00

Kammer & Reinhardt: Bisque socket head. Compo body. Open mouth. MARKS: SIMON-HALBIG 21/K star R. 24" $225.00

Kammer & Reinhardt: Bisque socket head. Open mouth. Sleep eyes. Head turns as doll walks. Compo body. Molded shoes. MARKS: SIMON-HALBIG/K star R/L 23. 25" $200.00

Kammer & Reinhardt: Bisque head. Sleep eyes. Open mouth. Compo body. MARKS: K star R/k 26. 19" $165.00

Kammer & Reinhardt: 1905. Bisque socket head. Open closed mouth. Painted eyes. Molded hair. Compo body. Baby with un-bent limbs. MARKS: K star R/Germany/28. 16" $285.00

Kammer & Reinhardt: Bisque socket head. Sleep eyes. Open mouth. Compo body. MARKS: SIMON-HALBIG 30/K star R/L. 32" $350.00

Kammer & Reinhardt: 1902. Bisque socket head. Open mouth. 3 teeth. Sleep eyes. Box with 3 extra heads. Compo body. MARKS: L/SIMON -HALBIG/K star R/30. 12" $250.00

Kammer & Reinhardt: 1905. Bisque socket head. Pierced ears. Open mouth. 2 teeth. Inset eyes. Tongue. Compo body. MARKS: SIMON-HALBIG/K star R/Germany/39. 22" $160.00

Kammer & Reinhardt: 1905. Bisque socket head. Pierced ears. Open mouth. 4 teeth. Sleep eyes. Compo body. MARKS: SIMON-HALBIG/K star R/Germany/40/. 24" $185.00

Kammer & Reinhardt: Called: "The Flirt". Bisque socket head. Open mouth. Sleep eyes. Side-to-side eye movement. Eyelids move. Compo body. MARKS: SIMON-HALBIG/K star R/Germany/42. 26" $350.00

Kammer & Reinhardt: 1909. Bisque socket head of a black. Closed mouth. Pouty. Painted eyes. Brown compo body. MARKS: K star R/101 32. 12" $950.00

Kammer & Reinhardt: 1909. Bisque socket head. Pouty. Closed mouth. Painted eyes. Molded hair. Compo body. MARKS: K star R/101 X/ 18. 14" $850.00

Kammer & Reinhardt: 1910. Considered a rare doll. Bisque socket head. Open closed mouth. Shy smiling boy called "Carl". Compo body. MARKS: K star R/107. 14" $1,100.00

Kammer & Reinhardt: 1912. Bisque socket head. Open closed mouth. 2 teeth. Tongue. Painted eyes. Flocked hair. Pouty. Compo body. MARKS: K star R/112 X/42. 16" $1,200.00

Kammer & Reinhardt: Early doll. 1902. Bisque shoulder head. Dimpled chin. Closed mouth. Painted eyes. Molded hair. Cloth body. Compo forearms. MARKS: K star R/114/Germany/11/0. 14" $1,300.00

Kammer & Reinhardt: 2 dolls from same mould. A girl and her baby sister. Called: "The Girl with a Doll". Bisque socket head. Closed mouth. Painted eyes. Pouty mouth. Compo body. MARKS: K star R/114. 10" $1,200.00

Kammer & Reinhardt: This is the boy edition. Bisque socket head. Closed mouth. Painted eyes. Pouty mouth. Mache body. Painted high shoes. MARKS: K star R/114. 10" $1,200.00

Kammer & Reinhardt: 1912. Bisque socket head. Closed mouth. Sleep eyes. Short compo body. MARKS: K star R/SIMON-HALBIG/115/60. 12" $1,100.00

Kammer & Reinhardt: 1912. Bisque socket head. Pouty. Closed mouth. Sleep eyes. Compo body. MARKS: K star R/SIMON-HALBIG/115 A/68. 12" $1,200.00

Kammer & Reinhardt: 1912. Bisque socket head. Open closed mouth. Tongue. Sleep eyes. Molded hair. 2 teeth. Compo body. MARKS: K star R/116/40. 14" $1,300.00

Kammer & Reinhardt: 1912. Bisque socket head. Open closed mouth. 2 teeth. Tongue. Dimples. Sleep eyes. Compo body. MARKS: K star R/116A/30. 14" $1,300.00

Kammer & Reinhardt: 1919. Bisque socket head. Open mouth. Flirty sleep eyes. Compo body. MARKS: K star R/SIMON & HALBIG/117n /38. 23" $265.00

Kammer & Reinhardt: 1912. Bisque socket head. Open closed mouth. 2 teeth. Tongue. Dimples. Sleep eyes. Compo body. MARKS: K star R/ SIMON-HALBIG/116 A/38. 14" $1,400.00

Kammer & Reinhardt: 1919. Bisque socket head. Closed mouth. Sleep eyes. Compo body. MARKS: K star R/117/38. 20" $1,300.00

Kammer & Reinhardt: 1919. Bisque socket head. Closed mouth. Sleep eyes. Compo body. MARKS: K star R/SIMON & HALBIG/117/68. 25" $1,400.00

Kammer & Reinhardt: Bisque socket head. Open mouth. Inset eyes. Pierced ears. Compo body. MARKS: HALBIG/K star R/43. 28" $225.00

Kammer & Reinhardt: 1905. Bisque socket head. Open mouth. 4 teeth. Sleep eyes. Pierced ears. Compo body. MARKS: SIMON-HALBIG/K star R/Germany/48. 29" $265.00

Kammer & Reinhardt: 1919. Bisque socket head. Open mouth. 2 teeth. Dimpled chin. Tongue. Dimples. Sleep eyes. Compo body. MARKS: K star R/SIMON & HALBIG/118/38. 20" $245.00

Kammer & Reinhardt: 1919. Bisque socket head. Open mouth. 2 teeth. No tongue. Compo body. Bent arms / legs. MARKS: K star R/SIMON & HALBIG/118 A/42. 23" $265.00

Kammer & Reinhardt: Bisque socket head. Open mouth. Sleep eyes. Tongue. Character. Compo baby body. MARKS: K star R/121.

Kammer & Reinhardt: 1920. Bisque socket head. Open closed mouth. 2 teeth. Tongue. 3 dimples. Flirty sleep eyes. Compo body. Bent limbs. MARKS: K star R/SIMON & HALBIG/121/40. 12" $225.00

Kammer & Reinhardt: 1920. Bisque socket head. Dimples. Open mouth. 2 teeth. Quiver tongue. Sleep eyes. HH. Compo body. Bent limbs. MARKS: K star R/SIMON & HALBIG/122/38. 14" $240.00

Kammer & Reinhardt: Bisque socket head. Open mouth. Sleep eyes. Tongue, that vibrates. Dimples. Character. Compo body. MARKS: K star R/122. 22" $300.00

Kammer & Reinhardt: Bisque socket head. Open closed mouth. Smile. Fat cheeks. Inset eyes. Compo body. MARKS: K star R/123. 18" $300.00

Kammer & Reinhardt: Bisque socket head. Open closed mouth. Smile. Inset eyes. Compo body. MARKS: K star R/124. 18" $300.00

Kammer & Reinhardt: 1924. Celluloid socket head. Open mouth. 2 teeth. Quiver tongue. Flirty sleep eyes of metal that move side-to-side. Hair lashes. Compo body. Voice box. MARKS: K star R/728/4/Turtle-mark/35. 20" $225.00

Kammer & Reinhardt: Bisque socket head. Open mouth. 2 teeth. Quiver tongue. Dimpled chin. Sleep eyes. Compo body. Bent limbs. MARKS: K star R/SIMON & HALBIG/128/36. 12" $200.00

Kammer & Reinhardt: Rare K&R googlie. Bisque socket head. Closed mouth. Smiling. Flirty googlie sleep eyes. Mohair. Compo body. Toddler. MARKS: K star R/131. 12" $750.00

Kammer & Reinhardt: 1923. Bisque head. Open mouth. Sleep eyes. Compo body. MARKS: Flapper K star R/138. 18" $225.00

Kammer & Reinhardt: Rare shoulder edition of mold no. 114, a pouty. Bisque shoulder head. Pouty. Closed mouth. Painted eyes. Kid body. Ball jointed arms and wrists. MARKS: 214/K star R. 14" $1,600.00

Kammer & Reinhardt: 1924. Celluloid shoulder head. Open mouth. 4 teeth. Inset eyes. Cloth body. Celluloid arms. MARKS: K star R/225 /Turtlemark. 18" $245.00

Kammer & Reinhardt: Bisque shoulder head. Open mouth. Sleep eyes. Kid body. Bisque forearms. MARKS: SIMON-HALBIG/K star R/246. 18" $160.00

Kammer & Reinhardt: Celluloid shoulder head. Open mouth. Sleep eyes. Wig. Double chin. Kid body. Celluloid hands. MARKS: K star R/ 255/Turtlemark. 18" $185.00

Kammer & Reinhardt: Rheinische Gummi 1924. Celluloid shoulder head. Open mouth. Inset eyes. Molded hair. Cloth body. Celluloid hands. MARKS: K star R/321/4Germany. 20" $225.00

Kammer & Reinhardt: 1920. Bisque socket head. Open mouth. 2 teeth. Quiver tongue. Sleep eyes. Compo body. Bent limbs. MARKS: K star R/SIMON & HALBIG/126/25. 21" $285.00

Kammer & Reinhardt: 1920. Bisque socket head. Open mouth. 2 teeth. Quiver tongue. Sleep eyes. A black. Brown compo body. Bent limbs. MARKS: K star R/SIMON & HALBIG/126/28. 16" $200.00

Kammer & Reinhardt: 1920. Bisque socket head. Open mouth. Sleep eyes. Tongue. Smile. Character. 2 teeth. Compo body. Bent limbs. MARKS: K star R/126. 12" $200.00

Kammer & Reinhardt: 1920. Bisque socket head. Open mouth. Sleep eyes. Molded hair. Tongue. Dimpled chin. Compo body. MARKS: K star R/127. 18" $285.00

Kammer & Reinhardt: Bisque socket head. Open mouth. 2 teeth. Tongue. Sleep eyes. Molded hair. Compo body. Bent limbs. MARKS: K star R/SIMON & HALBIG/127/36. 26" $350.00

KESTNER

14" Bisque shoulder head on kid body with bisque arms. Open mouth. MARKS: C/MADE IN GERMANY 7. $135.00

KESTNER

19" Socket head on fully jointed body. Sleep eyes/lashes. Open mouth with 2 upper teeth. MARKS: J.D.K./143. $285.00

KESTNER

30" Socket head on fully jointed body. Open mouth. Set eyes. MARKS: MADE IN/M GERMANY 16/146. $300.00

KESTNER

24" Socket head on fully jointed body. Set eyes. Open mouth. MARKS: K MADE IN GERMANY 14. $185.00

Kammer & Reinhardt: Bisque socket head. Open mouth. Sleep eyes. Flirty eyes. Compo body. MARKS: K star R/402 SH. 13" $195.00

Kammer & Reinhardt: Bisque socket head. Pierced ears. Dimpled chin. Open mouth. 4 teeth. Tongue. Sleep eyes. Compo body. Walks and turns head. MARKS: K star R/SIMON & HALBIG/403/48. 16" $265.00

Kammer & Reinhardt: Bisque socket head. Pierced ears. Dimpled chin. Open mouth. 4 teeth. Sleep eyes. Tongue. Compo walking body. MARKS: K star R/SIMON & HALBIG/403/50. 20" $295.00

Kammer & Reinhardt: Bisque socket head. Open closed mouth. Teeth. Painted eyes. Short Compo body. MARKS: K star R/442/45. 16" $185.00

Kammer & Reinhardt: Celluloid socket head. Open mouth. 4 teeth. Flirty sleep eyes of metal. Compo body. MARKS: K star R/717 65/ Turtlemark. 20" $225.00

Kestner, J. D.: Bisque socket head. Open mouth. Painted eyes. Painted hair. Baby compo body. MARKS: JDK/3 4/0. 9" $155.00

Kestner, J. D.: Bisque turned shoulder. Open mouth. Inset eyes. Kid body. Bisque forearms. MARKS: Made in /JDK Germany 8. 17" $135.00

Kestner, J. D.: Bisque socket head. Open mouth. Sleep eyes. Closed dome. Compo body. Bent limbs. MARKS: JDK 7. 16" $250.00

Kestner, J. D.: Bisque head. Open closed mouth. Closed dome. Sleep eyes. Compo body. Bent limbs. MARKS: JDK 7/Germany. 16" $250.00

Kestner, J. D.: 1912. Bisque socket head. Character. Closed mouth. Inset eyes. Painted hair. Compo body. MARKS: JDK 10/Germany. 21" $350.00

Kestner, J. D.: Bisque socket head. Open closed mouth. 2 low teeth. Inset eyes. Painted hair. Compo body. Bent legs. MARKS: JDK/Made in Germany 10. 12" $250.00

Kestner, J. D.: Brown Bisque socket head. Open mouth. Painted teeth. Sleep eyes. Brown mache body. MARKS: Made in/G Germany 11. 12" $350.00

Kestner, J. D.: Bisque socket head. Open mouth. Sleep eyes. Molded hair. 2 teeth. Character face. Floating tongue. Compo baby body. MARKS: JDK 11/Germany. 18" $315.00

Kestner, J. D.: Bisque socket head. Closed mouth. Inset eyes. Compo BJ body. MARKS: Made in/K Germany 14. 18" $315.00

Kestner, J. D.: Bisque socket & plate. Dimpled chin. Closed mouth. Sleep eyes. Kid body. Bisque forearms. MARKS: Made in/L Germany 15. 18" $400.00

Kestner, J. D.: Bisque socket head. Open mouth. 2 lower teeth. Sleep eyes. Painted hair. Compo body. Bent legs. MARKS: JDK/Made in Germany/16. 12" $350.00

Kestner, J. D.: 1892. Bisque socket head. Open mouth. Sleep eyes. Compo body, BJ. MARKS: Made in/N Germany 17. 17" $145.00

Kestner, J. D.: Bisque socket head. Open mouth. Sleep eyes. Painted hair. Compo baby body. MARKS: JDK 117. 25" $365.00

Kestner, J. D.: Bisque socket head. Open closed mouth. Inset eyes. Molded black hair. Compo body. Bent limbs. MARKS: Made in/JDK Germany/123. 20" $345.00

Kestner, J. D.: All bisque stiff neck. Closed mouth. Painted eyes. Mohair on closed dome marked "Kestner". 2 holes in dome. Molded shoes. MARKS: 158 5/0. $95.00

Kestner, J. D.: 1892. Bisque socket head. Dimpled chin. Open mouth. 4 teeth. Sleep eyes. Compo body. MARKS: Made in/P½ Germany 19½/171. 22" $145.00

Kestner, J. D.: 1910. Called "Gibson Girl". Bisque shoulder head. Long slender neck. Tilted nose. Closed mouth. Inset eyes. Kid body. Bisque forearms. MARKS: 2/0/172/Made in Germany. Kestner crown seal (body). 18" $1,500.00

Kestner. J. D.: 1892. Bisque socket head. Dimpled chin. Open mouth. 4 teeth. Sleep eyes. Compo body. MARKS: Made in/D Germany 8/174. 20" $200.00

Kestner, J. D.: 1910. Bisque socket head. Closed mouth. Sleep eyes. Compo body. MARKS: 187. 18" $450.00

Kestner, J. D.: 1892. Bisque socket head. Closed mouth. Sleep eyes. Compo body. MARKS: 0½/B½ Germany 6½/189. 18" $450.00

Kestner, J. D.: 1914. Bisque socket head. Open mouth. Sleep eyes. Laughing. Compo body. Baby. MARKS: Hilda c JDK Jr/190 Ges Gesch 1070/Made in Germany. 16" $650.00

Kestner, J. D.: 1910. Bisque shoulder head. Open mouth. Inset eyes. Fur eye brows. Hair lashes. Gussetted kid body. Bisque forearms. Cloth fore-legs. MARKS: 195 DEP 8 3/4/Made in Germany. 26" $200.00

Kestner, J. D.: 1896. Bisque socket head. Open mouth. Sleep eyes. Compo body. MARKS: Made in/L Germany 13/162. 22" $465.00

Kestner, J. D.: Yellow bisque socket head. Open mouth. Sleep eyes. Yellow mache body. MARKS: 164/Made in Germany. 18" $365.00

Kestner, J. D.: Bisque socket head on bisque shoulder plate. Open mouth. Sleep eyes. Kid body. 1896. MARKS: Made in/C Germany 7/164. 20" $225.00.

Kestner, J. D.: Bisque shoulder head. Open mouth. Sleep eyes. Kid body. Bisque forearms. MARKS: Made in Germany/166. 4. 20" $175.00

Kestner, J. D.: Bisque socket head. Open mouth. 4 teeth. Sleep eyes. Dimpled chin. Compo body. MARKS: C Made in Germany 167. 20" $325.00

Kestner, J. D.: 1892. Bisque socket head. Open mouth. 4 teeth. Sleep eyes. Compo body. MARKS: Made in/H Germany 12/168. 20" $185.00

Kestner, J. D.: 1892. Bisque socket & plate head. Open mouth. 4 teeth. Sleep eyes. Kid body/bisque forearms. MARKS: Made in/H Germany 12/129. 20" $185.00

Kestner, J. D.: Bisque turned shoulder head. Inset eyes. Kid body. Bisque forearms. MARKS: Made in/K Germany 135. 18" $185.00

Kestner, J. D.: 1892. Bisque socket head. Open mouth. Sleep eyes. Curls. Compo body. MARKS: Made in/L Germany 15/141. 22" $165.00

Kestner, J. D.: 1892. Bisque socket head. Open mouth. 4 teeth. Sleep eyes. Curls. Compo body. MARKS: Made in/O Germany 18/142. 22" $165.00

Kestner, J. D.: Bisque socket head. Open mouth. Sleep eyes. Compo body. MARKS: JDK 146. 22" $285.00

Kestner, J. D.: Bisque shoulder head. Open mouth. Sleep eyes. Kid body. Bisque forearms. MARKS: Made in/C½ Germany 7½/148. 20" $175.00

Kestner, J. D.: 1911. Bisque shoulder head. Open mouth. 4 teeth. Sleep eyes. Kid body. Bisque forearms. MARKS: 6 154 DEP. 17" $150.00

Kestner, J. D.: 1892. Bisque socket head. Open mouth. 4 teeth. Chin dimple. Sleep eyes. Curls. Compo body. MARKS: Made in Germany/J 3/4 DEP 13 3/4/156. 19" $175.00

KESTNER

18" Shoulder head. Open mouth.
Kid body with bisque forearms.
MARKS: 14. $150.00

KESTNER

17" Turned shoulder head. Sleep
eyes. Open mouth. Kid body with
bisque forearms. MARKS: D.
$225.00

KESTNER

19" Shoulder head with solid dome
and turned. Kid body with bisque
forearms. Sleep eyes. Open mouth.
MARKS: G $225.00

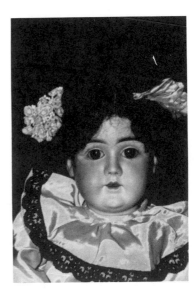

KESTNER

21" Socket head on fully jointed
composition body. Open mouth.
Sleep eyes/lashes. Molded brows.
MARKS: A MADE IN 5/GERM-
ANY 167. $145.00

52

Kestner, J. D.: Bisque shoulder head. Open mouth. Sleep eyes. Kid body. Bisque forearms. MARKS: JDK 7½ 148. 26'' $200.00

Kestner, J. D.: All-bisque stiff neck. 1895. Open mouth. Sleep eyes. Molded socks & shoes. MARKS: 150. 4. $85.00

Kestner, J. D.: Bisque socket head. Dimpled chin. Cheek dimples. Open closed mouth. 2 teeth. Tongue. Molded hair. Compo body. Bent limbs. MARKS: Made in/Germany/151/2. 15'' $250.00

Kestner, J. D.: Bisque socket head. Closed dome. Open mouth. Sleep eyes. Tongue. Mache body. Baby. MARKS: JDK 7½ 148/Germany. 23'' $185.00

Kestner, J. D.: 1892. Bisque socket head. Open closed mouth. Sleep eyes. Tongue. Dimples. Double chin. White bisque. Linon compo walking body. MARKS: JDK 152 C/Germany. 18'' $300.00

Kestner, J. D.: Bisque socket head. Open mouth. Sleep eyes. Wig with braids. Compo body. MARKS: JDK B6 167/Germany. 24'' $195.00

Kestner, J. D.: 1910. Bisque shoulder head. Open mouth. 4 teeth. Sleep eyes. Hair lashes. Fur brows. Short neck. Kid body. Bisque fore-arms. MARKS: 195 DEP 17/N Made in Germany. 19'' $165.00

Kestner, J. D.: Bisque socket head. Open mouth. Sleep eyes. Hair lashes. Fur brows. Compo body. MARKS: Made in/G Germany 11/196. 19'' $165.00

Kestner, J. D.: 1924. Celluloid shoulder head. Open mouth. Sleep eyes. Kid body. MARKS: JDK 201. 16'' $135.00

Kestner, J. D.: 1912. Bisque socket head. Open closed mouth. 2 teeth. Tongue. Sleep eyes. Compo body. MARKS: Made in Germany/211/ JDK/9. 18'' $300.00

Kestner, J. D.: 1892. Bisque socket head. Dimpled chin. Open mouth. 4 teeth. Sleep eyes. Compo body. MARKS: Made in/F½ Germany 10½/JDK/214. 16'' $235.00

Kestner, J. D.: Bisque socket head. Closed mouth. Smile. Inset eyes. Compo body. MARKS: Made in/G Germany 11/JDK/221/Ges Gesch. 18'' $495.00

Kestner, J. D.: 1892. Bisque socket head. Open mouth. Sleep eyes. Compo body. MARKS: Made in Germany/JDK/215/10. 18'' $265.00

Kestner, J. D.: Bisque socket head. Open mouth. Sleep eyes. Fur brows. Compo body. MARKS: JDK 216. 18'' $265.00

Kestner J. D.: 1892. Bisque socket head. Open mouth. 2 teeth. Sleep eyes. Double chin. Compo body. MARKS: Made in/C Germany 7/JDK /226. 20" $300.00

Kesnter, J. D.: Bisque shoulder head. Open mouth. Sleep eyes. Kid body. Compo arms & legs. MARKS: Made in Germany/JDK/235. 18" $225.00

Kestner, J. D.: 1914. Bisque socket head. Open mouth. 2 teeth. Sleep eyes. Compo body. Baby. MARKS: Made in/G Germany 11/237 15/ JDK Jr 1914 Hilda/Ges Gesch N 1070. 16" $650.00

Kestner, J. D.: Bisque socket head. Open mouth. 4 teeth. Inset eyes. Compo body. MARKS: JDK/241/Germany. 18" $235.00

Kestner, J. D.: 1892. Bisque (yellow) socket head. Open mouth. 2 teeth. Sleep eyes (slanted). Compo body. MARKS: Made in/F Germany 10/243/JDK. 16" $350.00

Kestner, J. D.: Bisque character socket head. Dimples. Open mouth. 2 teeth. Tongue. Sleep eyes. Mache body. MARKS: Made in Germany 2/0/247/JDK. 16" $300.00

Kestner, J. D.: Bisque socket head. Open mouth. Sleep eyes. Compo body. MARKS: Made in Germany/JDK 249. 16" $245.00

Kestner, J. D.: 1914. Bisque socket head. Open mouth. 2 teeth. Quiver tongue. Flirty sleep eyes. Smile. Compo body. MARKS: Made in Germany/JDK/257/34. 13" $225.00

Kestner, J. D.: 1919. Bisque socket head. Dimpled chin. Open mouth. 4 teeth. Sleep eyes. Compo body. Bent limbs. MARKS: JDK/260/Germany/39-44. 16" $300.00

Kestner, J. D.: Bisque socket head. Open mouth. Sleep eyes. Compo body. MARKS: Made in Germany/JDK 264. 18" $245.00

Kestner, J. D.: 1914. Bisque shoulder head. Open mouth. 2 teeth. Tongue. Inset eyes. Painted hair. Cloth body. Compo forearms. Pierced nostrils. MARKS: HILDA 1914 c/JDK 1914/Made in Germany/Ges Gesch 16/1040. 16" $650.00

Kestner, J. D.: 1914. A black toddler. Sleep eyes. Laughing. Head tinted brown. Brown compo body. MARKS: JDK Jr 245/Made in Germany/Hilda 1045. 16" $1,200.00

Kestner, J. D.: 1914. Bisque socket head. Sleep eyes. Laughing baby. Compo baby body. MARKS: Hilda c JDK jr/190 Gesgesch 1070/Made in Germany. 16" $650.00

Kestner, J. D.: Bisque socket head. Open mouth. 2 teeth. Tongue. Sleep eyes. Compo body. Bent limbs. MARKS: Hilda/Made in/N Germany 16/245/JDK 1914/5 Ges Gesch N 1070. 16" $650.00

Kley & Hahn: Bisque socket head. Sleep eyes. Compo body. MARKS: K&H/Kley & Hahn. 18" $235.00.

Kley & Hahn: Bisque socket head. Open closed mouth. 2 teeth. Tongue. Painted eyes. Molded hair. Compo body. Bent limbs. MARKS: K&H/142 2/0/Germany. 14" $395.00

Kley & Hahn: Bisque socket head. Open closed mouth. 2 teeth. Tongue. Compo body. Bent limbs. MARKS: K&H in banner/Germany/ 158 14. 16" $280.00

Kley & Hahn: Bisque socket head. Dimpled chin. Open closed mouth. 2 teeth. Tongue. Sleep eyes. Compo body. Bent limbs. MARKS: K&H in banner/Germany/167/9. 16" $225.00

Kley & Hahn: 1902. Bisque socket head. Dimpled chin. Open mouth. 4 teeth. Sleep eyes. Compo body. MARKS: 250/K H/Walkure/1½/Germany. 18" $185.00

Kley & Hahn: Bisque socket head. Open mouth. 2 teeth. Quiver tongue. Sleep eyes. Compo body. Toddler. MARKS: 266 680/44/K & H/Made in Germany. 22" $325.00

Kley & Hahn: Bisque shoulder head. Open mouth. Sleep eyes. Kid body. Bisque forearms. MARKS: K&H 1600 3/0/Germany. 18" $225.00

Kley & Hahn: 1902. Bisque socket head. Dimpled chin. Open mouth. 4 teeth. Sleep eyes. Compo body. MARKS: 282/K H/Walkure 3/Germany. 26" $265.00

Kley & Hahn: Bisque socket head. Closed mouth. Painted eyes. Dimples. Character face. Compo body. MARKS: Kley & Hahn/K & H 520. 16" $485.00

Kley & Hahn: Bisque socket head. Open closed mouth. Teeth. Sleep eyes. Painted hair. Compo body. MARKS: Germany/K & H/523/9. 16" $485.00

Kley & Hahn: Bisque socket head. Open closed mouth. Intaglio painted eyes. Painted hair. Character face. Compo toddler body. MARKS: Kley & Hahn/525. 12" $325.00

Kley & Hahn: Bisque socket head. Closed mouth. Painted eyes. Compo body. MARKS: K&H in banner/549/2/0/Germany. 16" $485.00

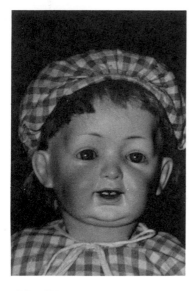

KESTNER

19" Socket head on 5 piece bent leg baby body. Sleep eyes. Open mouth/2 lower teeth. MARKS: MADE IN/GERMANY/J. D. K./ 211. $300.00

22" Socket head on fully jointed composition body. Open mouth. Sleep eyes. MARKS: MADE IN GERMANY/J. D. K./215. Fur eyebrows. $265.00

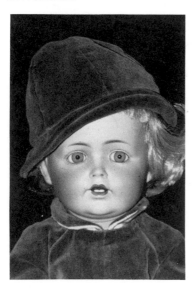

KESTNER

KESTNER

16" Socket head on bent leg, 5 piece baby body. Open mouth/ 2 lower teeth. MARKS: J. D. K. 257. $225.00

11" 5 piece bent leg baby body of composition. Sleep eyes. Open mouth with 2 upper teeth, which are painted. MARKS: K & H, in a banner/GERMANY/167-4. $325.00

Kley & Hahn: Bisque socket head. Open mouth. 2 teeth. Quiver tongue. Flirty sleep eyes. Compo body. Bent limbs. MARKS: 266-680/50/K&H /Made in Germany. 22" $285.00

Krauss, Gebruder: Bisque shoulder head. Pierced ears. Closed mouth. Inset eyes. Small crown opening. Kid body. Bisque forearms. MARKS: 38 GBR-K in sunburst 27. 18" $165.00

Krauss, Gebruder: Bisque socket head. Dimpled chin. Open mouth. Inset eyes. Mache body. Painted socks & slippers. MARKS: 44 GBR-K in sunburst 16. 16" $145.00

Krauss, Gebruder: Bisque shoulder head. Closed mouth. Inset eyes. Small crown opening. Kid body. Bisque forearms. MARKS: GBR-K in sunburst/38 27. 22" $450.00

Krauss, Gebruder: Bisque socket head. Open mouth. Inset eyes. Compo body. MARKS: 44 GBR-K in sunburst 29. 22" $180.00

Krauss, Gebruder: Bisque socket head. Dimple. Pierced ears. Open mouth. 4 teeth. Sleep eyes. Compo body. MARKS: 285/Gbr 165 K/ Germany/6. 20" $185.00

Krauss, Gebruder: Bisque socket head. Pierced ears. Open mouth. 4 teeth. Sleep eyes. Compo body. MARKS: Gbr 165 K/10/Germany. 20" $165.00

Recknagel, T.: Bisque head. Closed mouth. Sleep eyes. Googlie. Smile. Mache body. MARKS: R 3/0 A. 8" $395.00

Recknagel, T.: For L. Amberg & Son. Called "New Born Baby". Bisque head. Flanged neck. Closed dome. Bald. Open mouth. Sleep eyes. Cloth body. Compo arms. Baby. MARKS: L.A.&S/R A 241 5/0/Germany. 12" $95.00

Recknagel, T.: Bisque head. Sleep eyes. Compo body. MARKS: 21 Germany RA. 10" $85.00

Recknagel, T.: Bisque head. Closed dome. Closed mouth. Inset eyes. Molded hair & ribbon. Googlie. MARKS: R 46 A 12/0/Germany. 16" $125.00

Recknagel, T.: Bisque socket head. 2 holes over each ear. Open mouth. Sleep eyes. Compo body. MARKS: R 86 A/6/0. 18" $145.00

Recknagel, T.: Bisque head. Open mouth. Sleep eyes. Unusual character face. Compo body. MARKS: R A 1907. 20" $165.00

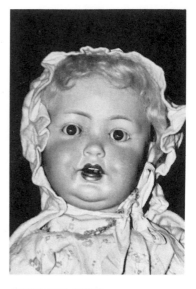

RECKNAGEL, T.

15" Socket head on fully jointed composition body. Open mouth/teeth. MARKS: 21/GERMANY/R 3/0 A. $125.00

REINECKE, OTTO

20" Socket head on 5 piece bent leg baby body of composition. Open mouth with 2 upper teeth. MARKS: P.M. 914/12. $185.00

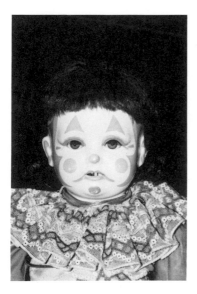

SCHOENAU & HOFFMEISTER

27" Socket head on fully jointed composition and wood body. Open mouth. Sleep eyes. All original clown. MARKS: S PB, in a star, H/170-4/GERMANY. $495.00

SCHUETZMEISTER & QUENDT

22" Socket head on composition fully jointed body. Open mouth. Sleep eyes/lashes. MARKS: 301. $295.00

Simon & Halbig: Bisque socket head. Open closed mouth. Tongue. Mache body. Baby. MARKS: S. H. 126. 16" $245.00

Simon & Halbig: An oriental. 1900. Olive bisque socket head. Open mouth. Inset eyes. Olive compo body. MARKS: S & H 139 DEP. 14" $365.00

Simon & Halbig: Bisque socket head. Open closed mouth. Painted eyes. Character face. Dimples. Compo body. MARKS: 151 S&H 1. 16" $350.00

Simon & Halbig: 1925. Bisque socket head. Open mouth. 2 teeth. Quiver tongue. Sleep eyes that move side-to-side. Compo body. Bent limbs. MARKS: SIMON & HALBIG/Made in Germany/156 75. 18" $265.00

Simon & Halbig: Bisque socket head. Open mouth. Sleep eyes. Compo body. MARKS: S & H 409/6. 18" $225.00

Simon & Halbig: Bisque socket head. Open mouth. 4 teeth. Sleep eyes. Compo body. MARKS: 540/Germany/HALBIG/S&H. 16" $200.00

Simon & Halbig: Bisque socket head. Dimpled chin. Open mouth. 4 teeth. Inset eyes. Compo body. MARKS: SIMON-HALBIG/S&H/550 /13. 18" $265.00

Simon & Halbig: Bisque socket head. Open mouth. Sleep eyes. Compo body. MARKS: 570 HALBIG S&H/Germany. 16" $200.00

Simon & Halbig. Bisque socket and shoulder plate. Closed mouth. Sleep eyes. Wig. Pierced ears. Kid body. Bisque forearms. MARKS: S 7 H 719 DEP. 16" $350.00

Simon & Halbig: Brown bisque socket head. Pierced ears. Open mouth. 4 teeth. Inset eyes. Compo BJ body. MARKS: S10H 739 DEP. 18" $265.00

Simon & Halbig: Brown bisque socket head. Open mouth. Inset eyes. Heavily painted lashes & brows. Compo body. MARKS: S&H 759 DEP. 18" $395.00

Simon & Halbig: Bisque socket head. Closed mouth. Sleep eyes. Pierced ears. Kid body. Bisque forearms. MARKS: S&H 769 DEP. 16" $400.00

Simon & Halbig: 1888. Bisque shoulder head. Closed mouth. Kid body. Bisque forearms. MARKS: S 4 H 905. 16" $450.00

Simon & Halbig: Bisque socket head. Pierced ears. Closed mouth. Lips parted. Inset eyes. Compo body. MARKS: S8H 929 DEP. 16" $450.00

Simon & Halbig: Bisque socket head. Pierced ears. Closed mouth. Lips parted. Inset eyes. Closed dome. Compo body. MARKS: S11H 939 DEP. 16" $450.00

Simon & Halbig: Bisque socket head. Open mouth. Teeth. Pierced ears. Sleep eyes. Compo body. MARKS: S12H 939 DEP. 18" $285.00

Simon & Halbig: Bisque socket head. Dimpled chin. Closed mouth. Sleep eyes. Compo body. MARKS: S2H 945 DEP. 16" $495.00

Simon & Halbig: Bisque socket head. Pierced ears. Dimpled chin. Closed mouth. Inset eyes. Lips parted. Closed dome. Holes. Compo body. MARKS: S6H 949 DEP. 16" $495.00

Simon & Halbig: Bisque socket head. Pierced ears. Dimpled chin. Open mouth. 4 teeth. Inset eyes. Compo body. MARKS: S14H 949 DEP. 20" $295.00.

Simon & Halbig: Bisque shoulder head. Dimples. Closed mouth. Inset eyes. Closed dome. Pink cloth body. Bisque forearms. MARKS: SH 2/950. 16" $400.00

Simon & Halbig: Bisque socket head. Closed mouth. Inset eyes. Molded hair. Pierced ears. Compo body. MARKS: 960 S H. 16" $450.00

Simon & Halbig: Bisque socket head. Closed mouth. Sleep eyes. Smile. Compo body. MARKS: 969 S&H. 16" $450.00

Simon & Halbig: Brown bisque socket head. Dimpled chin. Pierced ears. Open mouth. 4 teeth. Inset eyes. Mohair. Brown compo body. MARKS: S1H 1009/DEP/ST/Germany. 21" $295.00

Simon & Halbig: Bisque shoulder head. Pierced ears. Open mouth. 4 teeth. Sleep eyes. Kid body. Bisque forearms. MARKS: SH 1080 DEP 9. 18" $295.00

Simon & Halbig: Olive tint bisque head. Open mouth. Inset eyes. Slant eyes. Kid body. Bisque forearms. MARKS: S&H Oriental 1099. 16" $850.00

Simon & Halbig: Bisque socket head. Sleep eyes. Pierced ears. Compo body. MARKS: S&H 1109. 20" $365.00

Simon & Halbig: Olive bisque socket head. Open mouth. Sleep eyes. Slant eyes. Mache body. Wooden joints. MARKS: S&H 1129/Germany. 16" $800.00

Simon & Halbig: 1895. Bisque socket head. Open mouth. 4 teeth. Almond shaped eyes. Sleep eyes. Compo body. MARKS: 1159/Germany/HALBIG 7/S&H. 16" $300.00

Simon & Halbig: Bisque shoulder head. Closed mouth. Inset eyes. Pierced ears. Cloth body. Bisque arms. MARKS: S & H 4/01160. 16" $475.00

Simon & Halbig: Bisque shoulder head. Closed mouth. Inset eyes. Kid body. Bisque forearms. MARKS: S & H/1169. 16" $475.00

Simon & Halbig: Bisque shoulder head. Pierced ears. Open mouth. 4 teeth. Sleep eyes. Kid body. Bisque forearms. MARKS: 1170 SH 6½ D. 16" $395.00

Simon & Halbig: Olive bisque socket head of a Burmese. Pierced ears. Open mouth. 4 teeth. Sleep eyes. Olive compo body. MARKS: S&H /1199 6/0. 16" $850.00

Simon & Halbig: Bisque socket head. Open mouth. Sleep eyes. Pierced ears. Compo body. MARKS: 1248/SIMON & HALBIG/S&H 5. 16" $295.00

Simon & Halbig: Bisque socket head. Pierced ears. Open mouth. 4 teeth. Sleep eyes. Compo body. MARKS: SH 1249/DEP/Germany 8. 16" $395.00

Simon & Halbig: Bisque shoulder head. Open mouth. 4 teeth. Inset eyes. Pierced ears. Kid body. Bisque forearms. MARKS: SIMON & HALBIG/1280/DEP/Germany. 18" $325.00

Simon & Halbig: 1909. Brown bisque socket head. Closed mouth. Inset eyes. Pouty. Unhappy character face. Brown compo body. MARKS: S & H 1301/Germany. 16" $425.00

Simon & Halbig: Bisque socket head. Closed mouth. Inset eyes. Compo body. Adult female character. MARKS: S & H/Germany 1303/8½. 16" $485.00

Simon & Halbig: Bisque head. Open closed mouth. Inset eyes. Pointed nose. Pointed chin. Unusual female character face. Molded brows. Compo body. MARKS: S&H 1305. 18" $500.00

Simon & Halbig: Tan bisque socket head of an Oriental. Pierced ears. Open mouth. 4 teeth. Sleep eyes of almond shape. Tan compo body. MARKS: 1329/Germany/SIMON & HALBIG/S 4/0H. 12" $325.00

Simon & Halbig: 1907. Bisque socket head. Pierced ears. Open mouth. 4 teeth. Flirty sleep eyes. Compo body. MARKS: 1349/Jutta/S&H/11. 18" $245.00

Simon & Halbig: Brown bisque socket head. Pierced ears. Open mouth. Inset eyes. Broad flat nose. Mohair. Brown compo body. MARKS: 1358/Germany/SIMON & HALBIG/S&H/3. 16" $485.00

Simon & Halbig: Bisque head. Open mouth. Sleep eyes. Molded brows. Compo body. MARKS: SIMON & HALBIG/S & H/1388. 18" $275.00

Simon & Halbig: Bisque socket head. Open closed mouth. Sleep eyes. Compo body. MARKS: 1488/SIMON & HALBIG/15. 18" $495.00

Simon & Halbig: Bisque socket head. Open closed mouth. Sleep eyes. Painted hair. Compo body. Bent limbs. MARKS: 1498/SIMON & HALBIG/S & H 15. 18" $495.00

Simon & Halbig: Bisque head. Open mouth. Sleep eyes. Molded brows. Compo body. MARKS: S & H/Baby Blanche. 16" $245.00

Simon & Halbig: Bisque head. Closed mouth. Inset eyes. Pierced ears. MARKS: SIMON & HALBIG/S & H/IV. 14" $450.00

Simon & Halbig: Bisque shoulder head. Open mouth. 4 teeth. Sleep eyes. Kid body. Compo arms. MARKS: SH 1250/DEP/Germany 4. 18" $225.00

Simon & Halbig: Bisque shoulder head. Open mouth 4 teeth. Inset eyes. Adult. Kid body. Bisque forearms. MARKS: SH 1260 DEP/Germany 6. 18" $425.00

Simon & Halbig: Bisque socket head. Pierced ears. Dimpled chin. Cheek dimples. Open mouth. 2 teeth. Sleep eyes. Compo body. MARKS: S&H/1279/DEP/Germany 4. 18" $295.00

Simon & Halbig: 1905. Bisque socket head. Pierced ears. Dimpled chin. Open mouth. 4 teeth. Sleep eyes. Compo body. MARKS: 1078/Germany/SIMON & HALBIG/S&H/3. 36" $365.00

Simon & Halbig: 1905. Bisque socket head. Pierced ears. Dimpled chin. Open mouth. 4 teeth. Sleep eyes. Mohair. Compo BJ body. MARKS: S&H 1079/DEP/Germany/16. 18" $190.00

Simon & Halbig: Bisque socket head. Pierced ears. Dimpled chin. Open mouth. 4 teeth. Inset eyes. Compo body. MARKS: S7H 1009/ DEP/St/Germany. 16" $225.00

Simon & Halbig: Bisque socket & shoulder plate head. Pierced ears. Dimpled chin. Open mouth. 4 teeth. Inset eyes. Kid body. Bisque forearms. MARKS: S 8H 1009N/DEP/St/Germany. 18" $235.00

Simon & Halbig: 1890. Bisque shoulder head. Pierced ears. Dimpled chin. Open closed mouth. 4 teeth. Inset eyes. Blue felt cloth body. Bisque forearms. MARKS: SH 1010 DEP/2/0 E. 18" $195.00

Simon & Halbig: 1890. Bisque shoulder head. Dimpled chin. Pierced ears. Open mouth. 4 teeth. Sleep eyes. Gusseted Kid body. Bisque forearms. MARKS: S6½H 1010 DEP. 18" $195.00

Simon & Halbig: 1890. Bisque socket head. Pierced ears. Open mouth. 4 teeth. Inset eyes. Compo body. MARKS: SH 1019 8½ DEP/Germany. 20" $225.00

Simon & Halbig: 1890. Bisque socket head of tamborine player (mechanical). Pierced ears. Open mouth. 4 teeth. Flirty inset eyes. Mache body on music box. MARKS: SH 1039/3 DEP. 14" $550.00

Simon & Halbig: 1905. Bisque socket head. Pierced ears. Dimpled chin. Open mouth. 4 teeth. Flirty sleep eyes. Compo walking body throws kisses. MARKS: 1039/Germany/SIMON & HALBIG/S&H/ 10½. 20" $285.00

Simon & Halbig: 1890. Bisque socket head. Pierced ears. Open mouth. 4 teeth. Flirty sleep eyes. Compo body. MARKS: SH 1039/HALBIG/ 11. 18" $265.00

Simon & Halbig: 1895. Bisque shoulder head. Pierced ears. Open mouth. 4 teeth. Inset eyes. Cloth body. Kid upper arms. Bisque forearms. MARKS: SH 1040 6 DEP. 23" $195.00

Simon & Halbig: Bisque socket head. Open mouth. Inset eyes. Cloth body. Wooden arms. MARKS: S H 1059 DEP/2. 23" $210.00

Simon & Halbig: Bisque shoulder head. Closed mouth. Inset eyes. Pierced ears. Kid body. Bisque hands & feet. MARKS: S H 1060 /Germany. 23" $210.00

Simon & Halbig: Bisque shoulder head. Open mouth. Sleep eyes. Pierced ears. Kid body. Bisque forearms. MARKS: S H 1069 DEP/2. 30" $350.00

SCHUETZMEISTER & QUENDT

9" Solid composition body. Jointed arms & legs. Closed mouth "Belton" type with 2 holes on top of head. Original trunk & wardrobe. MARKS: S Q 20. $495.00

SIMON & HALBIG

19" Shoulder head on kid body with bisque arms. Open mouth. MARKS: S 79 H 1010 DEP. $190.00

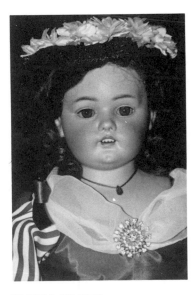

SIMON & HALBIG

26" Shoulder head on kid body with bisque arms. Sleep eyes. Open mouth. MARKS: S & H 1040. $225.00

SIMON & HALBIG

32" Shoulder head on kid body with bisque arms. Sleep eyes/ lashes. Open mouth. Molded brows. MARKS: SIMON HALBIG/1080. $350.00

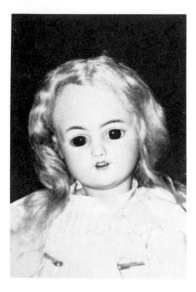

SIMON & HALBIG

17'' Socket head on fully jointed body. Open mouth sleep eyes. MARKS: 1249/DEP/GERMANY/ SANTA/6½. $295.00

SIMON & HALBIG

19'' Socket head on fully jointed body. Open mouth. Sleep eyes. Flirty. MARKS: S & H/1279 /SANTA. $295.00

SIMON & HALBIG

29'' Socket head on fully jointed body. Sleep eyes. Open mouth. MARKS: 1348/JUTTA/SIMON & HALBIG. $245.00

STEINER, EDMUND

32'' Socket head on fully jointed composition and wood body that is marked: Jumeau. Open mouth. Sleep eyes/lashes. MARKS: MAJ-ESTIC/18/GERMANY/REGAL. $350.00

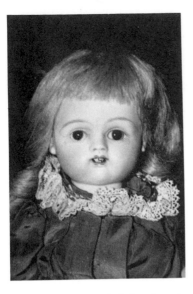

9½" All bisque with jointed neck, shoulders & hips. Feet are bare with modeled toes. Open mouth /2 rows of teeth. MARKS: 4, on head. $375.00

6½" All bisque with jointed shoulders & hips. Sleep eyes with lashes. Open mouth. MARKS: 180/J.D.K. $200.00

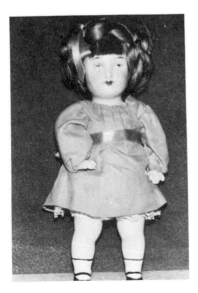

6½" All bisque with one piece body & head. Painted eyes to side. Painted on shoes & socks. $65.00

8" All bisque with one piece body & head. Open/closed mouth. Sleep eyes. MARKS: 11. $75.00

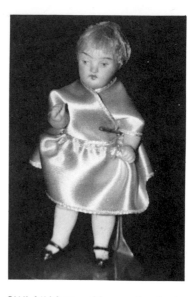

4" All bisque with one piece body
& head. Sleep eyes. Molded on
shoes & socks. $75.00

3½" All bisque with one piece body
& head. Painted eyes. Painted on
shoes & socks. MARKS: GER-
MANY. $65.00

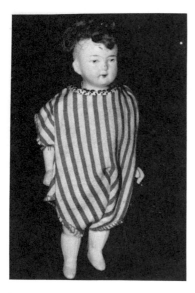

6" All bisque with one piece body
& head. Modeled on shoes & socks
but left unpainted. Painted eyes.
Closed mouth. MARKS: S 114.
$65.00

4" All bisque with modeled on
clothes. Modeled ribbon in hair.
Pin jointed arms only. $115.00

4½" All bisque Bonnet doll with pin jointed shoulders only. MARKS: 162, on back. $125.00

6½" All bisque with jointed shoulders only. Painted on shoes & socks. MARKS: MADE IN/JAPAN. $75.00

4" All bisque with jointed shoulders only. Painted black from waist down with painted brown shoes. MARKS: JAPAN. $30.00

5½" All bisque with one piece body & legs. Molded pink ribbon in hair. Painted on shoes & socks. MARKS: JAPAN. $35.00

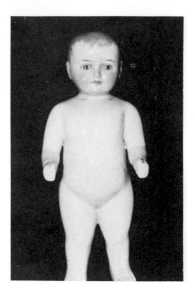

6'' All bisque Frozen Charlotte with gold painted on shoes. Original clothes. $65.00

6'' China All bisque Frozen Charlie. $100.00

3½'' China Frozen Charlotte all bisque. MARKS: 8. $45.00

5½'' All bisque with jointed arms & legs. Molded painted hair and eyes. MARKS: 1414/GERMANY. $75.00

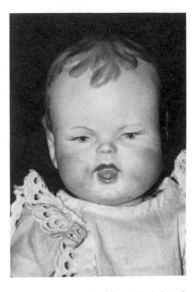

5" All bisque baby with curved baby legs. One piece body & legs. MARKS: JAPAN $20.00

9" All bisque baby with jointed neck, shoulders & hips. Molded -painted hair. Painted eyes. MARKS: none. $95.00

2½" All bisque "nodder" with jointed neck. MARKS: JAPAN $37.50

3" All bisque "nodder" with jointed neck. MARKS: JAPAN. $37.50

4" All bisque "nodder" with jointed neck. MARKS: JAPAN. $37.50

5" All bisque in riding habit. No
joints. MARKS: JAPAN. $25.00

4" ANDY GUMPS. All bisque
nodder with jointed neck. MARKS:
ANDY GUMP, on back. $67.50

6" "BIMBO" All bisque with jointed shoulders only. MARKS: BIM-
BO, on back. JAPAN, on foot.
$35.00

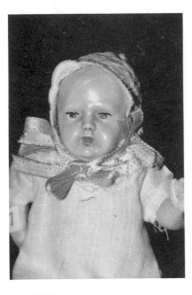

VICTORIA

5½" All celluloid baby with one piece body & head. Made by Victoria Toy / Novelty Co. 1920. MARKS: V. CO., in circle/USA. $18.00

CHASE

27" CHASE stockenette play doll. $185.00

FULPHER

15" Bisque head baby with 5 piece composition baby body. Sleep eyes. Open vertical mouth/2 upper teeth, MARKS: MADE IN/USA. $245.00

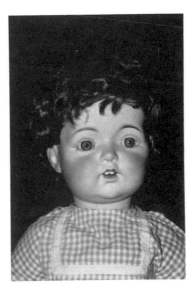

FULPHER

22" Bisque head on fully jointed composition toddler body. Open vertical mouth/2 upper teeth.

MARKS: MADE IN/USA. $285.00

72

19" Celluloid socket head on 5 piece composition baby body. Flirty, sleep eyes; lids drop down over the eyes. Open mouth/2 upper teeth. MARKS: K star R/728/17/43/46. $225.00.

3½" All celluloid with one piece body & head. Original. $8.00

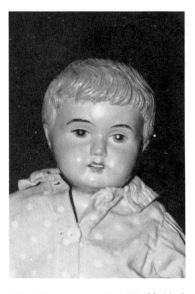

5" All celluloid. Fully jointed. All original. $8.00 each.

16" All painted celluloid. Molded hair. Painted eyes. Open mouth. MARKS: Turtlemark/SCHULZ-MARK/NO. 40. $87.50

73

19" Brown glass eye china. Ears exposed. Cloth body with parian limbs. $1,895.00

19" Pink luster china with BROWN painted eyes. Cloth body with leather arms. 1850. $550.00

21" Bald/wigged china. Kid body with leather arms. $995.00

13" China with molded on scarf and grapes. Kid body with leather arms. $1,350.00

13" China with hair pulled back. Cloth body with China limbs. $365.00

10½" Waterfall hairdo China with molded black bow in back of head. Cloth body with china limbs. $375.00

10½" Variation of the Jenny Lind. Cloth body with china limbs. $395.00

20" Full bangs with brush stroke marks. Cloth body & china limbs. $365.00

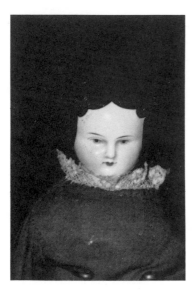

13" Blue painted eyes and down turned head. MARKS: none. $165.00

28" China with large painted pale blue eyes. Modeling at base of throat. $265.00

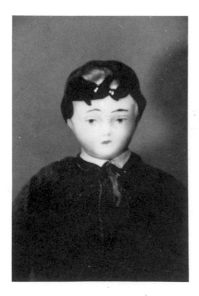

10" China boy with side part and 2 curls on forehead. Kid body with leather arms. Ca. 1850. $400.00

29" China boy. Ears exposed. Cloth body with china limbs. $450.00

11″ China with blue painted eyes with pupils that are large. $125.00

17″ Blonde china with fine modeling. Kid body with china limbs. $235.00

15″ Blonde china with ears exposed. Cloth body with china limbs. $265.00

16″ Light brown "Curly Top" china. Cloth body with china limbs. $485.00

20" China with ears partly exposed. Brush strokes at temples. $260.00

12" Pink luster china of the 1860's Cloth body with china limbs. $225.00

17" Adelade Patti china with brush marks at temples. Partly exposed ears. Cloth body with china limbs. $350.00

25" China with peaked hairdo. Cloth body with china limbs. $350.00

25" China with blue painted eyes. High peak & white hair part. MARKS: GERMANY $200.00

14" China with partly exposed ears. MARKS: none. $145.00

18" China. With full bangs and ears exposed. $200.00

17" China with hair pulled back into a bun. $400.00

30" Cloth body and legs. "Whitish" composition arms. Composition head with molded hair. Painted eyes. MARKS: ELEKTRA, on head. $75.00

28" Bent cloth stuffed legs. Gauntlet composition arms. Painted features. Smiling mouth with dimples. $65.00

RIGHT: 23" Cloth body with composition head & limbs. Molded hair. Painted eyes. MARKS: F. LEFT: 19" Cloth & composition. Molded hair with loop for ribbon. $75.00 each.

30" Cloth excelsior filled body, upper arms & legs. Composition head & lower limbs. Painted eyes & lashes. MARKS: none. $32.00

27'' Bed Doll. Composition shoulder head. Compo. full arms and
lower legs. Cloth body. Painted
eyes with long hair lashes. MARKS:
W K/IN. Designed by the Violette
F. Wright for Flapper Novelty Co.
1924. $35.00

34'' Bed Doll. Composition head,
arms & legs. Mohair wig. Painted
eyes/lashes. $30.00

16'' All composition with red glued
on mohair wig. Painted blue eyes.
MARKS: C. D. Made by Century
Doll Co. $35.00

12'' Campbell Kid. All composition. Painted features. Made by
Horsman in 1948. $65.00

2″ White dress. Pink necklace. Yellow hat with pink/green flowers. Dark blonde hair. One arm behind back. MARKS: 5331. $30.00

2½″ Pink dress. Gold trim/blue sash & ribbon. Light brown hair. Good skin tones. MARKS: GERMANY $40.00

3″ White molded on dress. Deep red necklace. Black hair. Excellent skin tones. MARKS: GERMANY $35.00

2½″ Flesh tones. Orange bonnet with black ribbon. MARKS: 22480 $30.00

2" Green dress with white inset front piece. Grey hair. Pink/white fan. MARKS: can't read. $15.00

3¼" Pink dress and rose. Yellow hair. MARKS: JAPAN, inside. $8.00

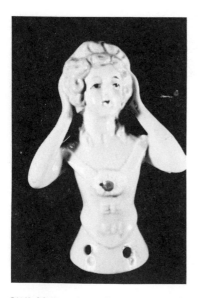

3½" Yellow hair. Pink dress with orange center to bow. MARKS: MADE IN JAPAN $12.00

3½" White with rose checks on dress. Orange bow & hat. Blue feather, cuffs & collar. MARKS: JAPAN $8.00

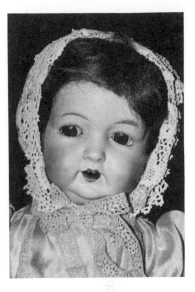

13" Shoulder head on kid body. Bisque lower arms. Sleep eyes. Open mouth. MARKS: 5/ /NIPPON. $125.00

22" Bisque socket head on composition 5 piece baby body. Open mouth/2 upper teeth. MARKS: 22/ /JAPAN. $135.00

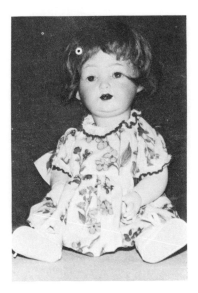

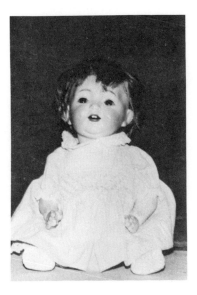

13" Socket head on toddler body. Wrists are jointed. Molded closed mouth with 2 painted upper teeth. MARKS: $165.00

11" Socket head on 5 piece baby body. Open mouth/2 teeth. Sleep eyes. MARKS: /JAPAN/2. $135.00

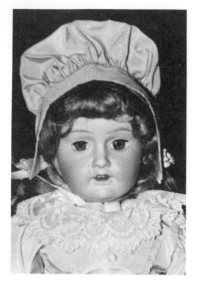

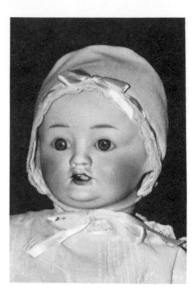

21" Socket head on fully jointed composition body. Set eyes/lashes. Open mouth. MARKS: 5/ /NIPPON. $185.00

20" Socket head on 5 piece baby body. Sleep eyes. Open mouth with two upper teeth. MARKS: F Y/20/5/NO. 70018. $135.00

17" Socket head on fully jointed composition body. Sleep eyes. Open mouth. MARKS: F Y/No. 70018/200. $100.00

7" Chinese Boy and Girl. Bisque hands. Composition and mache bodies, arms and legs. Swivel neck. Open crown, human hair. Pierced nostrils "breathers". Original silk clothes, jacket marked Japan inside. MARKS: 11-06 $20.00 each.

18" Thin mache Sicily Creche figure with inset glass eyes. $1,000.00

14" woman & 15" man. Creche figures. Wood limbs. $285.00 each.

19" Painted black hair. Painted blue eyes. Cloth body with leather arms. Made by L. Greiner. $350.00

21" Painted black hair & eyes. Cloth body with leather arms. Made by L. Greiner. $350.00

5" Mache head. Blonde molded hair. Painted eyes. $85.00

6" Negro mache of 1885. Large painted eyes. Jointed shoulders & hips. $235.00

20" Stuffed oil cloth body, and limbs that are disc jointed. Stitched fingers. Mache head with inset glass eyes. Open mouth. Human hair wig. MARKS: none. $45.00

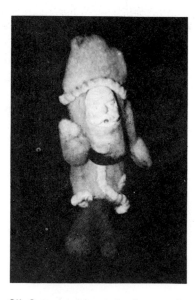

3" Cotton with mache face mask. Germany $25.00

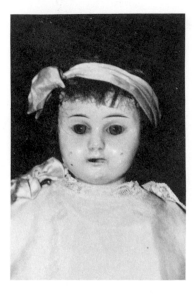

23" Metal shoulder head. Sleep eyes. Open mouth. Cloth and leather body. MARKS: GERMANY/5 $65.00

13" Metal head with sleep eyes and closed mouth. Cloth body. MARKS: none. $45.00

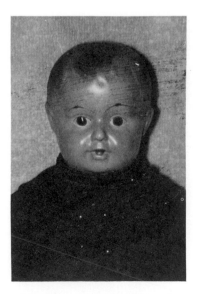

16" Metal head boy. One piece shoulder plate with 2 sew holes front & back. Painted blue eyes. Cloth body, bisque lower arms, leather legs. MARKS: none. $85.00

12" Metal head with cloth body & bisque ½ arms. Open mouth/4 teeth. MARKS: GERMANY 1½, on back. MINERVA/helmet, on front. $75.00

19" Parian with applied wreath of Dresden flowers and a blue luster ribbon and tassel. Cloth body with parian limbs. $895.00

12" Swivel neck Parian. Cloth body with parian arms. MARKS: 2½, on back. $165.00

20" Countess Dagmar with blue enamel "paperweight" eyes. Cloth body with parian limbs. $400.00

18" Blonde Parian with ringlet curls. Cloth body with leather arms. MARKS: 1056 no. 7 $325.00

10″ Parian of 1860 hairstyle. Cloth body with china arms. $295.00

10″ Parian boy. Cloth body with bisque arms. $175.00

12″ Parian with molded pink bow. Blue trimmed collar. Cloth with stone bisque limbs. $185.00

13″ Blonde Parian with blue glass eyes. Shoulder head on cloth body with parian limbs. $435.00

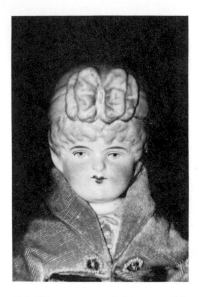

14" White bisque with modeled on bonnet & bow. Cloth body with white bisque limbs. $295.00

13" White "stone" bisque with molded on bonnet. Applied decoration on shoulder. Cloth body with leather arms. $185.00

16" White "stone" bisque with modeled bonnet and bow. Cloth body with white bisque arms. $340.00

12" White bisque with painted blue eyes. Cloth body with white bisque arms & legs. $80.00

8" Schoenhut clown. $65.00

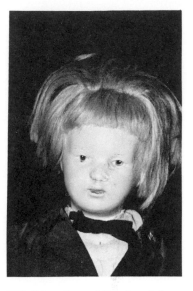

15" Schoenhut with painted features and wig. $225.00

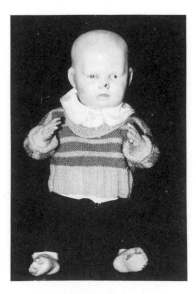

15" Schoenhut with bent baby limbs. Painted features. $200.00

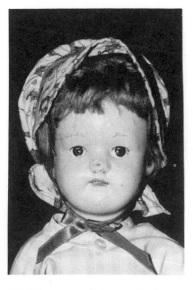

16" Schonehut. Fully spring jointed. Decal eyes. Painted mouth & teeth. $240.00

12" All wood peddlar doll. Painted hair and eyes. Original clothes. $35.00

15" All wood with a layer of mache. Painted features. Jointed arms & legs. $60.00

15" Joel Ellis Springfield wood with metal hands & feet. Jointed shoulders & hips. $500.00

9" All wood that is laminated plywood. Jointed at shoulders only. Glass eyes. MARKS: THINGS/PLY-THINGS. $18.00

INDEX

97

LETTER & NUMBER

SYMBOL INDEX

 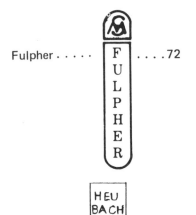